CREATURELY LOVE

CARY WOLFE, SERIES EDITOR

*(continued on page 166)*

# CREATURELY LOVE

How Desire Makes Us More and Less Than Human

DOMINIC PETTMAN

posthumanities 42

*University of Minnesota Press*

*Minneapolis*

*London*

Portions of chapter 2 were previously published as "When Lulu Met the Centaur: Photographic Traces of Creaturely Love," *NECSUS European Journal of Media Studies* 5, no. 1 (2015): 127–44; reprinted with permission of *NECSUS*. An earlier version of the Epilogue was published as "Wings of Desire," *Cabinet*, no. 55 (Fall 2014): 34–39.

Published by the University of Minnesota Press
111 Third Avenue South, Suite 290
Minneapolis, MN 55401-2520
http://www.upress.umn.edu

Printed in the United States of America on acid-free paper

The University of Minnesota is an equal-opportunity educator and employer.

22   21   20   19   18   17        10   9   8   7   6   5   4   3   2   1

Library of Congress Cataloging-in-Publication Data

Names: Pettman, Dominic, author.

Title: Creaturely love : how desire makes us more and less than human / Dominic Pettman.

Description: Minneapolis : University of Minnesota Press, 2017. | Series: Posthumanities ; 42 | Includes bibliographical references and index.

Identifiers: LCCN 2016015359 | ISBN 978-1-5179-0120-2 (hc) | ISBN 978-1-5179-0121-9 (pb)

Subjects: LCSH: Love. | Desire.

Classification: LCC BD436 .P424 2017 | DDC 128/.46—dc23

LC record available at https://lccn.loc.gov/2016015359

She would like to think the gods admire, however grudgingly, our energy, the endless ingenuity with which we try to elude our fate. *Fascinating creatures,* she would like to think they remark to each other over their ambrosia; *so like us in many respects; their eyes in particular so expressive; what a pity they lack that je ne sais quoi without which they can never ascend to sit beside us!*

**J. M. COETZEE,** *ELIZABETH COSTELLO*

# CONTENTS

# PREFACE

Suppose we considered the love of Antony and Cleopatra, Romeo and Juliet, or Swann and Odette from the perspective of the popular media-friendly genre "animals in love." Here the lovers are not "people" per se but merely two creatures enamored with each other, like the two otters holding hands while floating in the water in the famous viral video. We might then treat a forbidden love between the Capulets and the Montagues like one of those novelty stories where an elephant is inseparable from a dog or a pig from a hedgehog. While this comparison may appear willfully perverse or facetious, denigrating humanity's most cherished state to something bestial, it has the benefit of jolting us out of certain lazy, even dangerous habits of mind, specifically, those assumptions concerning ourselves and the exceptionalism of our capacity for affection and being affected.[1]

The traditional distinction essentially boils down to this: animals experience *attraction,* by instinct, whereas humans experience *love,* which is instinct supplemented and complicated by cultural forces (law, art, language, custom, psychology, and so on).[2] New approaches to "the animal question," however, have troubled this simplistic and self-flattering distinction. Moreover, earlier depictions of passionate encounters, in contrast to the great anthropocentric engineering project of the three major monotheisms, approach any boundary between human and animal to be fluid, provisional, and easily erased (as we find in Ovid, among many others). The pages that follow thus argue two contrary positions simultaneously, attempting to make peace with the contradiction by the closing pages (noting that the conflict is more of an inevitable paradox, created by the lover's discourse itself, than a dialectic seeking resolution). On one hand, humans and animals at the very least potentially share many characteristics, from the biological to the phenomenological, including the capacity to love and be loved. There is an affective continuum linking humans and animals, manifest in all sorts of ways. On the other hand, it is delusional and ethically precarious to collapse all distinctions between species and simply say "animals are just like us" or "we are just like animals." These are the Scylla and Charybdis any meditation on "the human" and its various creaturely others must navigate.

One way to do so—perhaps the only way—is to acknowledge that there is no metaphysical gulf separating so-called Man from dogs, monkeys, or starfish but a long historical–technical distinction without essential or definitive implications. The human is then considered not an animal body blessed with a human soul—a kind of superanimal—but instead a bundle of physical, psychical, and sociological mechanisms, shot through with prehuman, inhuman, posthuman, and infrahuman tendencies and trajectories. From this perspective, animals are also bundles of potentialities, including, in some cases, for language and other capacities we have traditionally classified as human. (As William Burroughs once said, "human" is an adjective, not a noun.) The challenge is to resist the old habit of "ontological apartheid": equating species with specific bodies and then quarantining them from each other. (For instance, where humans have sapience and animals merely sentience.)

Humans are emphatically not then some kind of Aristotelian augmented animal: a loving animal as well as a political or rational one. Rather, they are—we are—a specific instance of life composed of different vectors (DNA, ethnic patterns, mediatic influences, etc.) that themselves co-compose other creatures in the current global ecology. (As Nabokov said of people, we could possibly say of all creatures, "We are all anagrams of each other.") But again, the task is to resist collapsing all life onto one Great Plane—the flat ontology of much current Continental philosophy—while also avoiding a default relapse into familiar hierarchical positions: the Great Chain of Being. Love is thus the name we give to the precoded, even overdetermined, attractions between not only "people" but also animals (and even, possibly, things).[3] There is an elective affinity involved, of sympathies, inclinations, valences.

As humans, we like to think that we love the other for their unique *humanness,* whether we find this incarnate in a smile, a silhouette, or a soul. The beloved is always encountered *in media res,* embedded in a cultural context, from the clothes they wear to the comportment of their body to the words they are speaking, if only through their eyes. Animals enjoy none or little of this. But the present text works diagonally against this grain, acknowledging its truth—as far as it goes—but also arguing that what we love in the beloved precedes and exceeds that abstract element we call the human. Love thus makes us both more and less than human. Whether it is the texture of the beloved's skin or hair, their singular scent, the way they drool in their sleep, the way they eat with their mouth open, or the way they are trapped within their own *umwelt* of semiotic disinhibitors, we love the creaturely in the other, as much as their humanity. In fact, we could go so far as to insist that love is not a human phenomenon at all but an attempt to make the other admit, under a type of passionate interrogation, that they are *not* human; never were human; were trying to fool us with their distracting, sophisticated ways. Love would thus be the litmus test which we all fail—and, in doing so, ironically succeed. For we all suspect, at various levels of consciousness, that we are not really human. Or not only human. And it is that twilight between love and lust known as desire that we unmask the pretension of species-being (as Nietzsche knew so well).

Which is all to say that this little book is only about bestiality in the sense that two humans making love are (always already) animals engaged in sexual intercourse, whether they are literally between the sheets or not.

# INTRODUCTION

*On the Stupidity of Oysters*

"The stupidity of oysters is legendary." So reads the opening sentence of Paul Reboux's (2004) *Animals and Love,* a book virtually unknown outside of France and rarely read within it. This minor comedic gem—written in a dry, ironic style—presents a bestiary of different creatures, sketching the sordid or pathetic details of their diverse attempts to find (or avoid) companionship. So what makes the oyster so stupid? "They are incapable of tasting the pleasures of love. Such a prospect only makes them yawn" (7). As if to illustrate the master-motif of missed encounters between the sexes, Reboux writes, "This oyster here, the male, lets his seed slip through the shell which stands ajar. This one there, the female, captures it without wishing to, inside the water that she imprisons in her own shell as it closes. The seed unites with the ovum here where it recently dropped. The ovum accommodates this newcomer. Impregnation occurs" (7). Ironic, then, that the sexual experience for these famously aphrodisiacal creatures is so apathetic and so solitary. Reboux's little aphoristic sketches are so amusing because they refuse the sentimentality with which we usually view "the birds and the bees," trading the saccharine narrative voice-overs of nature programs for a sardonic critique. Hence, "sparrows are only mediocre lovers. . . . Without any preliminaries, without caresses, they place in contact a little patch of themselves against a little patch of the female. That's it" (9–10). As for cows? Well, they are "capable of emotion. But the bull is a bureaucrat. There are few lovers who are so swift. Just enough time to come and go. When they are so visibly talented, when they possess such a robust body, this air of power and majesty, they need to justify their reputation better. The bull gives a mediocre and too fugitive pleasure. He feels far too little of himself" (10–11). As for the melancholic bear? "He knows how to live the conjugal life. His den is, in fact, two or three kilometers from that of his spouse" (12). There is something refreshing in such an irreverent voice, because it humanizes the animal, depicting other creatures as not such perfect figures of natural grace after all. (Something countless viral videos do today—amateur animal versions of *America's Funniest Videos*.)[1]

My own book takes a leaf from Reboux, not in ironically *humanizing* the animal but in proposing that love is intrinsically and inescapably "creaturely." Given that there is no ready consensus about what love is— nor is there ever likely to be—this claim is often in sharp contrast to, and on occasion in harmonious concord with, the most cherished voices in the Western tradition, depending on which authority we are currently paying attention to. It is relatively safe to say, however, when pressed, that the received wisdom believes love to be something specific to the human, whether we figure it as the noble feeling above and beyond mere impulse or appetite or as the dark siren song of passion, jealousy, and obsession. Animals, so the thinking goes, with their simple spirits and instinctual limitations, are incapable of experiencing Eros in all its complex manifestations. They are "water within water" (Bataille)—so at one with their environment that they cannot conceive of a foreground for the love-object to inhabit. The rough consensus is that although attraction, even desire, can be found in some of the "higher" animals (chimps, dolphins, dogs, etc.), most behavior that may on the surface appear as affectionate is more instinctual—the friendly face of the selfish gene.[2] (Of course, some heartless scientists will say the same about humans.) The purpose of the present study is not to somehow prove, or even argue, that animals are in some sense our erotic equivalent; rather, it is to identify and unpack the creaturely, nonhuman "heart" of our own lover's discourse. What we love about the beloved, I submit, is not (only) his or her humanness, whatever that might be, but their "animal side" (to borrow a phrase from Jean-Christophe Bailly [2011]). That is to say, in the marketplace of big ideas, we almost always put our thumb on the scales when measuring the significance of our own species.

Love can be defined in various ways, none of them *definitive* but some certainly more compelling than others.[3] Roland Barthes (1990), for instance, insists that the narratives of love, on which the phenomenon depends, inhabit a prescripted "image repertoire" that we inhabit from our enamored ancestors. Love is thus a particularly legible map for navigating the popular imaginary (or what we might call the Spectacle, or the mediated condition).[4] For Niklas Luhmann (2010), love is the word we use for the historical "codification of intimacy"—which itself ushers in different epochs according to the range of possibilities available for the self in relation to wider society. One of the more salient features of modern love, according to Luhmann, is its dependence on a model of indirect communication—and the ongoing expectation that a lover should "understand" the beloved, without explicit discussion. Intimacy is thus nourished by virtue of the mutually unacknowledged subtexts of couplehood. Alain Badiou (2012) argues that love is a very special form of exhibiting "fidelity to the event," in which an isolated being resolves to co-create, and sustain, a world of desire with an exceptional Other (whose random idiosyncrasies nevertheless "represent" humanity, taken as a whole). Love is the knowingly quixotic quest to render the radical contingency of the erotic encounter into a profound, *retrospective* inevitability or fate. ("I could have fallen in love with *anyone*. And I did! *You!*")

At this point the reader may well ask, however, whether it is advisable to make a distinction between *love* and *desire* (even as my title and subtitle treat them as synonyms). Well, yes. And no. Laurent Berlant (2012) has convincingly argued, in her brilliant gloss on Lacan titled *Desire/Love*, that love is what happens to desire when it is obliged to adhere to the cultural forms and understandings that have been explicitly designed to capture and control this unstable force or phenomenon. Love is thus the congealed aspect of a more free-floating desire once it has been rendered conventional, overdetermined, scripted. Desire thus describes those types of affective yearning or sympathy that precede, or manage to escape, the diminished and diminishing options of what Berlant calls "the love plot" (in the sense of both *story* and *conspiracy*)—"so bound up in institutions like marriage and family, property relations, and stock phrases." For Berlant, "desire visits you as an impact from the outside, and yet, inducing an encounter with your affects, makes you feel as though it comes from within you" (6). Love, in other words, provides the processing power for making the anonymous pulsions of desire (what Lacan called *extimacy*) feel intimate and unique. Simply put, love is presented by Berlant as only *one form* that desire takes: indeed, the most compromised and limited form, in terms of predetermining the ways you can express such desire. And yet, it is also the form of desire that is most visible and legible to those around you, since we have all been taught from a young age to recognize its signs and signals and to respond accordingly. Thus Berlant notes that "even in its most conventional form, as 'love,' desire produces paradox.

It is a primary relay to individuated social identity, as in coupling, family, reproduction, and other sites of personal history; yet it is also the impulse that most destabilizes people, putting them into plots beyond their control as it joins diverse lives and makes situations" (13). In other words, the erratic properties of desire are nestled and smuggled within the lover's discourse, threatening to blow up any romantic situation at a moment's notice. "Regardless of how it is experienced by the desiring subject," Berlant writes, "desire can overwhelm thought, shatter intention, violate principles, and perturb identity. It is as though desire were a law of disturbance unto itself to which the subject must submit to become a subject of her own unbecoming" (26). Love, in contrast, at least attempts to provide a cultural corset, mental map, and emotional life coach, to ensure that the ambivalences and contradictions inherent in the subject's attractions and enthusiasms don't become too obvious to anyone involved in the plot. Love is thus "the theatrical or scenic structure of normative fantasy" (69), which itself rations the erotic into manageable parcels by "spacing out desire" (both temporally and geographically).[5] In short, "love is the misrecognition you like, can bear, and will try to keep consenting to" (106).

For Freud (1955), the desire–love distinction is not so important, since these are both descriptions and expressions of the libido. The rose, so to say, would smell as attractively (or repulsively) pungent no matter what we were to call it:

> Libido is an expression taken from the theory of the emotions. We call by that name the energy, regarded as a quantitative magnitude (though not at present actually measurable), of those instincts which have to do with all that may be comprised under the word "love." The nucleus of what we mean by love naturally consists (and this is what is commonly called love, and what the poets sing of) in sexual love with sexual union as its aim. But we do not separate from this—what in any case has a share in the name "love"—on the one hand, self-love, and on the other, love for parents and children, friendship and love for humanity in general, and also devotion to concrete objects and to abstract ideas. Our justification lies in the fact that psycho-analytic research has taught us that all these tendencies are an expression of the same instinctive impulses; in relations between the sexes these impulses force their way towards sexual union, but in other circumstances they are diverted from this aim or are prevented from reaching it, though always preserving enough of their original nature to keep their identity recognizable (as in such features as the longing for proximity, and self-sacrifice). We are

of opinion, then, that *language has carried out an entirely justifiable piece of unification in creating the word "love" with its numerous uses,* and that we cannot do better than take it as the basis of our scientific discussions and expositions as well. (89–90, emphasis added)

Love is, for both Freud and Berlant, a sublimated form of libidinal attachment. But for the father of psychoanalysis, this is all the more reason to use a constellation of terms to explain the overlaps, connections, and complicities involved in their expression within various psychosocial registers. Otherwise, we risk making somewhat arbitrary—and ultimately moralistic—distinctions between "love," on the one hand, and "desire," on the other. (The distinction remains, whether the former is deemed more noble, or more feeble, than the latter.)

Whether desire emerges within our breast because we lack what we think we need to become a fully-fledged person (Lacan) or because of a more "positive"—yet impersonal—inclination toward new arrangements between beings and materials close at hand (Deleuze), the word *love* will likely continue to be considered by many theorists to be a sentimental bandage, covering the violence of attachments both sought and sundered. Yet Freud's impulse to use the terms interchangeably brings conceptual benefits (even as it frustrates our inner taxonomist). For one thing, such a promiscuous practice acknowledges the single or shared origin of passionate attachments (or the energy—both psychic and physical—devoted to achieving them). The Christian distinction between *eros* and *agape* continues today, in secular and popular forms. But there may be wisdom in throwing them back together in the same hotel room and seeing how they get along, for they have much to teach each other. (Indeed, the ancients, who coined such terms in the first place, use them with rather wanton abandon in their own erotic fables.)

Always inspired by the pagans, Bataille called the profound metaphysical urge to achieve physical "continuity" with another human being *eroticism*. "Love," for this thinker, is simply a more intense version of erotic experience, far more so than mere "physical desire." In Bataille's system, love is not Berlant's cooling operation toward the heat of desire but the flame beneath that threatens to excite a psychic explosion. We can see, then, the different ways these key terms have interlaced in the Western literature on the relationship between eros and civilization. (And my own book is, admittedly, focused on this tradition, both to address its unfortunate legacies stretching into today and to note the moments where the

Occidental discourse on love and desire posited possible promising directions not taken—some of which may not be too late to backtrack to and explore.)

Love today is still primarily coded as spiritual. And desire is still coded as physical. Yet they inform each other, yin and yang style, down through the centuries. For Badiou (2012, 36), "love proves itself by permeating desire." And yet, for him, desire (in the physical sense) must still be present for this proof to be delivered:

> Surrendering your body, taking your clothes off, being naked for the other, rehearsing those hallowed gestures, renouncing all embarrassment, shouting, all this involvement of the body is evidence of a surrender to love. It crucially distinguishes it from friendship. Friendship doesn't involve bodily contact, or any resonances in pleasure of the body. That's why it is a more intellectual attachment, and one that philosophers who are suspicious of passion have always preferred. Love, particularly over time, embraces all the positive aspects of friendship but love relates to the totality of the being of the other, and the surrender of the body becomes the material symbol of that totality. (36)

Vilém Flusser (2014, 51), for his part, puts things more directly: "love, without any sexuality, becomes that saccharine sham that has as little to do with real love as the recitation of scripture has to do with real faith." But whether or not we personally subscribe to the notion that one must get naked to show love for another, we do well to recognize the very blurry boundaries between the physical and what we might call the existential modes of attraction. Both love and desire (as opposed to mere drive or want) tend to force a re-membering of Being. This is why the experience shocks us so profoundly into feeling born anew, into a new world. "Desire is immediately powerful," writes Badiou, "but love also requires care and re-takes" (85). Conversely, desire is replenished by returning to the source. "'Tell me again that you love me' . . . 'Say it better.' And desire begins again" (86).

For the purposes of the present book, love and desire are considered to form a Möbius strip. Consequently, when I use one term, I am also implicating the other. (Where humans are concerned, one will rarely be found without the other, since "mere desire" will always occur in the vacuum created by a perceived lack of love. Just as nature abhors a vacuum, culture abhors physical intimacy, untouched by the lover's discourse.) In the following pages, love is thus figured as the privileged and reflexive form of the transitivity of being. It is at once a physical and metaphysical *leaning toward*, in the hope of recognition, encounter, and exchange. Love is the overdetermined sign of a focused and intensified acknowledgment of alterity: the compulsory attempt to create a feedback loop between individuals, which itself reconfigures those individuals as more than atomistic selves.[6] And although, to gesture to Lacan, there may not be a true, verifiable "relationship" in such an encounter, there are, within the space love opens up, at least two parallel relationships within this (non?)relationship.

Do animals experience love? Do they enjoy and/or suffer *jouissance*? Do they have the symbolic wherewithal to upgrade mere attraction into the aesthetic exception of love? These are not questions addressed in this book. To hazard a guess would be precisely that, to hazard a guess, without even the benefit of rigorous ethological observation. Rather, the following pages ask a constellation of questions, such as, Do those animals that call themselves human experience love? And if so, what does this key term and the expression of this experience—in the different media of writing, image making, movement, and music—tell us about our now undeniable animal inheritance? What does it say about our posthuman context, perhaps even destiny?

We tend to use the term *creature* for another person either to belittle them or revere them. This wide spectrum is revealing. On one hand, the creature is a figure of abjection—a mere animal or even monster—whereas on the other, it is a description of alien, perhaps even ethereal fascination or beauty. When used in contempt, the term has a distancing effect, designed to highlight the assumed gap between person and creature. But when used in admiration, it suddenly bridges such a gap or even places it in the opposite direction, away from the animal and toward the angel. Although most of us acknowledge our animal aspect *conceptually*—as a matter of muted fact or science—very few do so in a consistent or coherent manner in our everyday lives. We prefer to think of it as a vague Darwinian heritage, or something we casually transcend on a day-to-day basis, unless war, lust, or desperation forces us to lapse "back" into an animal state. Such habits of thought mean we rarely acknowledge the creaturely basis of our existence: ideologically, ethically, politically, affectively, or aesthetically. These are the modes that really touch us and that constitute the rudder of our thoughts and actions. And these are the modes that we jealousy guard for our own species.

From this perspective, the dominant and official narrative of Western culture has been an elaborate disavowal of our creaturely life (a narrative produced by what Giorgio Agamben calls the "anthropological machine"). Of course such narration is made up of many voices, some of whom question or subvert the *Homo sapiens* party line. And it is to these voices that we shall attend in the following pages—voices that admit that, on a certain level, *all* eyelashes are eyelashes, whether they are connected to a pig, a dog, a giraffe, a human, or an elephant; voices that recognize a profound kinship, within or despite vast and undeniable biological and ontological differences. To focus on the possible shared nature of being is a strategic choice; it is also a scandal in some quarters (even today, when triumphant humanism has been largely hollowed out by the "ego-bruises" delivered by scientific discoveries, technological innovations, and our own shameful histories). It allows the prefix in words and ideals like *com*munity, *com*munication, and *com*passion. For you cannot aspire to these without a basis for being-with, being-together, or having something in common. The ongoing and tacit cultural refusal to acknowledge animal others as having "the right to exist" as something other than standing reserve or nonhuman resources has cast a persistent shadow over human endeavor, even as calls for vegetarianism on sympathetic grounds have been heard since at least the time of Epicurus. In the wider scheme of things, St. Francis is the exception rather than the rule.

To glimpse the creature in the human beloved is to see through the self-fulfilling myth of the human itself: that provisional, asymptotic, hypothetical destination we chase but never reach. It is to undress the beloved: to remove layer upon layer of self-serving species propaganda. Yet it is not merely to expose the cartoonishly didactic figure of "the naked ape"— the beast beneath the beauty—but to thrill in the intelligence that pulses under our skin, beneath our eyes, and within our gestures (an intelligence shared by other creatures, albeit in very different ways). To behold the creaturely aspect of ourselves is not to simply "reduce" the human to the animal—or, conversely, to "raise" the animal up to the human—but to ponder what Bernard Stiegler (2015, 55) calls "the-non-inhuman-within-inhuman-being." It is to rejoice in the miraculous singularity of the being that one is with, while also understanding the profound universality represented by his or her presence: the fact that the embraced body is but a temporary refuge for a universe of generic, genetic materials. It is this impossible thought—this antihumanistic paradox—that creaturely love exhibits and enacts.

# 1   DIVINING CREATURELY LOVE

The question remains: *which* creature are we talking about when we talk of creaturely love? Is it a term that secretly unites all the terrestrial beings that have been divorced from each other by evolutionary time? Does it diagram an essential connection, despite radical difference (for instance, "the living")? Or are there as many different types of creatures as there are species? Is it, in other words, legion? The word *creature* may sound to our modern ears as if it has wild, musky, perhaps even monstrous connotations. In fact, this term brings with it heavy religious cargo. The phrase "creaturely love" has traditionally been associated with theological debates around the enigmatic nature of affection between God, the Supreme Creator, and His key *creation*, Man. Indeed, this predominantly Christian discourse—defined by Augustine and revised many centuries later by Aquinas—continues to thread its way into discussions of human eros and the possibility for transcendence.[1] No doubt a different book, dedicated entirely to this topic, would be necessary to do such a history justice. But for our purposes here, it suffices to note that for Augustine, creaturely love is lacking the spiritual surplus essential to the holy life. It "is generally needy and poor, so that its outpouring makes it subordinate to the objects that it loves" (1982, 26). Our own earthly desires are merely distractions from the path of righteousness, all too often leading to sin. This is because our hearts (and loins) tend to maintain a strict focus, and we become fixated on this or that person or idea rather than having a more diffuse understanding of the World-as-Eros-as-Godhead. (It is in this sense that the phrase "heavenly creature" is something of an oxymoron, from the Augustinian perspective.)

Creaturely love manifests through specific attachments, which goes against the grain of the biblical commandment to "love thy neighbor" (that is to say, *all* our fellows). Thus the creaturely love-object is a fallen target of our emotional cathexis—an unworthy decoy that makes us forget that "we long to fly back to the bright home, to the rapturous embrace [of God] we spurned and left behind" (O'Connell 1996, 40). Only through such a noncreaturely—or more-than-creaturely—embrace do we have a chance to be resurrected without the stain of our kind. As 2 Corinthians 5:17 tells us, "if any man *be* in Christ, *he is* a new creature" (KJV). On the other hand, given that we were created in God's image, our love for one another is not *entirely* to be disparaged. For Augustine, such affection needs to be recognized as such: as a risky opportunity for transcendent love. The human body thus becomes the potential portal to God's ineffable affection. Human or creaturely love is thus tasked with avoiding the fetish of the temporary flesh, or even the *individual* soul nestled within such flesh. Only insofar as the beloved is an avatar of God is she or he truly lovable. But yes, granted, in such terrestrial desires lie the seeds of potential blessed bliss, provided the lover understands that the true beloved is God himself.[2] (Indeed, according to Augustine, the Great Architect taps into our human love to create enough wattage to power the light of the universe: "Night never falls while the Creator is not forsaken by the creature's love" [2012, 177].)

But despite the ongoing hope that love between earthly creatures could be deflected toward its rightful place in heaven, Augustine was essentially a pessimist and felt increasingly discouraged about our ability to nurture these seeds of bliss en masse.[3] Indeed, it was Augustine who cemented the doctrine of "original sin as transmitted through sex" (Tracy 2005, 100). No question, the divine aspect of creaturely love receives one of its greatest blows in the Garden of Eden, when Eve eats of the Tree of Knowledge at the behest of one of God's other creations, the snake. Henceforth, the favored one—Man—must navigate his fallen position within the context of original sin: a foundational crisis structured not only by gender but also by interspecies complicity. Adam, Eve, and the serpent constitute the first problematic love triangle, a *ménage à trois* that displaces the *ménage* so that the domestic nature of home is never definitively settled or located. Henceforth, in the West at least, there is always a nonhuman third term hissing and whispering in the wings or the bushes, trying to thwart our rapprochement with the Lord.

For Aquinas, creaturely love was somewhat more nuanced, because there are dangers in ascribing sinful properties to something that exists due to God's sculptural or animation skills. Love is thus, in all its forms, a transitive system, considered by God as nothing other than God Himself. As one commentator puts it, "because grace perfects nature . . . the natural love of God for God's own sake must be stronger than the creature's love of self, otherwise the completion of a creature's love would be selfish" (Keck 1998, 107). Grace is that medium that renders creaturely love (always already) sacred. So "creaturely love" in the theological and scholastic tradition is that which is not (yet) redeemed. It is "temporal" and material, thus mortal: human all too human. It thus requires the blessing and recognition of God to reconnect into the perfect feedback loop of grace.

Certainly fine-grained theological debates resist easy summary.[4] And the celebrated exegetes—in their tacking this way and that, depending on the argument and the text involved—provide enough material for many centuries of meta-interpretation. This is why "creaturely love" can never be completely disentangled from its religious roots—monotheistic and messianic. Nor can it be easily rescued from the long tradition of authorized attempts to provide and police our love-objects and to channel our libidos into sanctioned channels and images, at prescribed intensities and in ordained forms and languages.[5] In modern times, the phrase "creaturely love" spiked in the middle of the nineteenth century (according to Google Ngram), just as Darwin was assembling the most comprehensive and vigorous attack yet on the notion of a metaphysical conception of intelligent design. The creature was an especially important figure to the Victorians, caught between the old world of passive incarnation and the brave new world in which we are quickly becoming prosthetic gods ourselves, with the neo-Promethean capacity to create life. In Mary Shelley's classic novel *Frankenstein* (published in 1818, a year before the birth of Queen Victoria), we witness an important shift in definition, so that it is the creature itself—the monster—who seeks love from its maker, like an abandoned orphan: an allegory for a culture preparing itself to announce the death of God on behalf of the human race as a whole. A century later, as the Great War shattered any lingering notions of building a global city of God on the principles of grace, *caritas*, and civilization, the term "creaturely love" practically disappeared from the lexicon, only to resuscitate itself mid-century, in a kind of semi-embalmed state, until the present day.

For the contemporary theologian Thomas Jay Oord (2010, 199), "when we regard God as a necessary cause for all creaturely existence, it is plausible to speculate that all creatures rely on God when choosing to love outsiders and enemies, those near and dear, and even themselves. God is an objective though invisible agent, and creatures perceive divine causality, God's causal activity serves as the ground and inspiration for all creaturely love. We love, because God first loves us." The layperson might speculate, however, on God's rather tautological motivations in creating creatures capable of creaturely love (or capable of love at all, even and especially for Him). What is it about monotheistic divinities—even beyond Christianity—that seem to crave absolute affection? This is in marked contrast to the gods of Ovid (although the God of the New Testament did indeed "know" a mortal, Mary, in the biblical sense). To the sceptic, such an implicitly conditional operation—"I create you in order to love me properly"—smacks of a needy Pygmalion emotional logic, even of divine loneliness. There is something of the pet owner here, writ large. For the pet owner expects unconditional love in return for the living conditions provided (even the condition of life itself, in the case of rescue dogs). Perhaps there are traces of the divine libidinal economy in *all* earthly loves, since we "created" our own partners, in a sense, by bringing them into existence through our amorous attention. Just as they created us.

But even if we bracket the religious resonance of the term, the creature still confounds. Indeed, to list the definitions of the word *creature* from the *Oxford English Dictionary* is to be confronted with the complexity, even contradiction, embedded in the expression: "a created thing or being," "a material comfort," "a human being; person, or individual," "a fellow-creature" (i.e., a desirable person), "a reprehensible or despicable person," "an animal, often as distinct from a person," and even "a puppet." As with many key signifiers, it can denote opposed states of existence, sometimes at one and the same time. For two and a half millennia, the many-faced subject—*creature*—has been coupled with the notoriously elusive verb—*love*. No wonder we feel like we've been chasing our tails!

The chapters that follow provide a belated sketch of such tail chasing, primarily in that nebulous, fertile zone where literature and philosophy meet and proceed to awkwardly court each other. I begin with the moderns and modernists—Nietzsche, Salomé, Rilke, Balthus, Musil, and Proust—before moving swiftly backward in time to the premoderns—Fourier, Fournival, and medieval folktales. I then take a further leap back to the pagan poet of the creature par excellence, Ovid, before returning to the present to finish with a few meditations on animal attachment in two films: Kelly Reichardt's *Wendy and Lucy* and Spike Jonze's *Her*. This structure allows us first to establish the key themes of creaturely love, along with the stakes involved, from the relatively recent past. The modernists were asking certain important questions about the human more eloquently than we do today, by virtue of forging new styles and idioms by which to ask them. (Today, such styles are rather exhausted or muffled, through overuse and repeated appropriation.) But the modernists are also close enough to us, temporally speaking, to deliver messages from their own time as something more than merely esoteric, romantic, or strangely sincere. So it pays to revisit some of the scenes and texts of their initial attempts to ask vital existential questions—particularly those concerning our own raison d'être as a species—afresh, before these became calcified by the culture industries or rendered quaint, naive, or pointless by the many agents who actively work to discourage such questions being asked anew today (questions such as, What is it about you that I love: your humanity, or something before or beyond that? If indeed I adore your "humanity," how might we define that in a positive way? How might our humanity differ from our animal heritage or legacy? How does the understanding of human sexuality influence our sense of species-being? How does gender skew the discussion between sexual beings, and to what extent is gender itself a human fabrication, or a creaturely concern? Finally, how do we remain human while making the hybrid beast-with-two-backs? Indeed, *should* we remain human at such a moment? What lessons are there to draw, if any, from the intense but fleeting erotic encounter that we can bring with us into normal, social, public life?).

Once these key themes and questions have been established, then we will be in a stronger position to go back in time, in the following pages, and demonstrate how the longer Western tradition has been, in certain important senses, an unbroken (yet often stuttering or contradictory) conversation with itself about the complicated kinship between humans and animals. The ordering of chapters is thus as much about theme or figure as it is to do with chronology—even as we follow the dramatic three-act structure of the prolonged present, the extended flashback, and then the return to present day. Although my intellectual instinct is usually to draw attention to the original and essential role of technology in areas of life that seem to be vigorously defending themselves *against* the intrusion of media or machines (e.g., love), for this project, I have decided to "bracket off" the explicit question of technics until the concluding chapters. I do this for two main reasons: the first is to test my own thinking when obliged to resist depending on its default mode, and the second is to foreground the importance of the animal figure in the canonical Western discourse of love and desire (while continuing to insist—in sotto voce, as it were—that the animal, human, and machine are all intimately connected corners of the same "cybernetic triangle"). As the patient reader will discover, however, in the closing pages of the book, technology begins to encroach once more, with some of today's most sophisticated machines reminding us that we can no longer assume that a lover or companion—or even a creature per se—is necessarily organic or mortal at all.

# 2  HORSING AROUND

*The* Marriage Blanc *of Nietzsche, Andreas-Salomé, and Rée*

> Nietzsche . . . arranged a photograph of the three of us, in spite of strong
> objections on the part of Paul Rée, who suffered throughout his life from a
> pathological aversion to the reproduction of his features. Nietzsche, who
> was in a playful mood, not only insisted on the photo, but took a personal
> hand in the details—for example the little (far too little!) cart, and even the
> touch of kitsch with the sprig of lilacs on the whip, etc.

So recalls the original Lulu—Lou Andreas-Salomé (1990, 48)—of one of
the most surreal and intriguing images we have of the infamously imposing and brooding philosopher.[1] Here Nietzsche is "horsing about" with
Lou herself and the reluctant, heartsick poet Rée. In that golden summer of 1882, this self-described "trinity" were living together in the Swiss
mountains near Lucerne, where the photo was taken. They were in the
midst of a *marriage blanc*, held temporarily together with the formidable and fragile bonds of intellectual Eros. Lou hoped their love triangle
would yield unprecedented spiritual and mental fruit, which is why she
insisted on sexual abstinence, believing this would help avoid distracting
complications. (No wonder Nietzsche felt somewhat frisky and wished
to sublimate his desires into an allegorical assemblage of Hegelian fetish play.) As one translator and commentator notes of the photographic
oddity, "the backdrop is composed of a scene with a tree, a bush, and the
Jungfrau mountain. The expression on Nietzsche's face could be read as
visionary; Lou and Rée scarcely betray amusement. The whole picture,
with the artificiality of the studio, the coexistence of indifference (Rée),
stiltedness (Lou), and posed devotion to an inner image (Nietzsche),
seems more grotesque and uncanny than it does amusing" (Mitchell, in
Andreas-Salomé 1990, 153).[2]

·  15

The image is all the more remarkable when we consider the famous fable of Nietzsche's own insanity and the event that was said to trigger it: witnessing the cruel beating of a horse in a Turin square, prompting a fit of sympathy that effectively broke the great man's brain (albeit one already softened by syphilis). Looking at this bizarre visual echo of Nietzsche's virtually unknown "playful" side—seven years before the breakdown—it is difficult not to see a proleptic affinity between himself and an abused beast of burden, no matter how kitsch Lou's whip appears in the picture. There is an irony infused in the image, bridging the two moments— somewhere between the poetic, cosmic, and biographic.

While the debate continues concerning the degree to which this famously tragic moment is apocryphal or not, the story has become a primal scene for Western philosophy. (Most recently, for instance, it provides the structuring absence of Béla Tarr's remarkable film *The Turin Horse* [2011].) The power of the scene rests on a further fatal irony: Nietzsche, the great Zarathustrian warrior of the right and mighty, is undone by a tsunami of pity inspired by a single beast. (Had not the same man, in a book called *Genealogy of Morals*, warned against such tender sympathies as a Trojan Horse, bearing yet more moralistic slaves into the city?) How to read this anomalous moment of empathy and compassion in the light of his un-Samaritan perspective on ethics? Did he empathize with the horse, seeing its will-to-power bridled and injured so? Did he see the creature as a proxy for his own imminent fallen and harassed state? Was there pure projection or some kind of mutual communication? Was there a telescoping of his vivid past on to the agoraphobic present, linking the mounted cavalry with his own pagan Calvary? Such questions haunt the margins of this photograph.

Nietzsche's work has a strong totemic aspect to it, enlisting figural and symbolic animals for his countermoral system—eagles, lions, asses, and so on. Interestingly, given the ostensible source of his meltdown, horses did not feature, even though they seem ready-made to serve as avatars of nobility and transcendence, leaping over old resentments and kicking slave mentality in the teeth. However, there are a few cameo moments when horses appear in his life and writing. In 1867, for instance, Nietzsche signed up for one year of voluntary service with the Prussian artillery division in Naumburg. He woke up at 5:30 every morning to muck out the manure in the stables and groom his own steed. In a letter to a friend penned at this time, Nietzsche (1996b, 32) writes, "I like the riding lessons best. I have a very good-looking horse, and people say I have a talent for riding. When I whirl around the exercise area on my Balduin, I am very satisfied with my lot." However, in March of the following year, the young man had a riding accident, leaving him exhausted and unable to walk for months, and he subsequently returned to the library chair rather than the saddle. Later, in *Human, All Too Human*, Nietzsche (1996a, 292) would write, "A good posture on a horse robs your opponent of his courage and your audience of their hearts—why do you need to attack? Sit like one who has conquered!" In the same text, Nietzsche represented the historical will, inspired by "the light of genius," as a horse ready to "break out and leap over into another domain" (111).

Of course that other giant of Germanic letters, Freud, also viewed the horse as a totemic creature,[3] which often featured in neurotic or psychotic narratives revolving around what he called "anxiety-animals." In the famous case of Little Hans, who was five years old, the paralyzing fear of horses stemmed—or so Freud insisted—from displaced ambivalence concerning the father and his intimidating "widdle." The father–horse chimera is at once magnificent, dreadful, enviable, and fascinating. Indeed, this case prompted Freud to look at children's self-representation in an entirely new light, via modern-day totemism, inflected through the oedipus complex. Ultimately, Freud would use the horse as his own symbol for the id itself: a powerful yet unruly animal, requiring the ever-straining harness of the superego to function with disciplined direction.[4] For Freud, then, *all* humans are in some sense centaurs. Thus there is something inherently erotic or libidinal about actual horses, given that the animalistic "lower" half is powered by the id.[5] And this is why they are one of the primary totems for libidinal economics in general.[6]

If animals are good to think with, as Claude Lévi-Strauss famously maintains, then *mythical* creatures help us to challenge the more common lines of such thinking. The centaur has a privileged figural and symbolic power in the popular imaginary, its hybrid form embodying the Janus-aspect of phenomena. In *Human, All Too Human*, Nietzsche writes, "If anyone wanted to imagine a genius of culture, what would the latter be like? He would manipulate falsehood, force, the most ruthless self-interest as his instruments so skillfully he could only be called an evil, demonic being; but his objectives, which here and there shine through, would be great and good. He would be a centaur, half beast, half man, and with angel's wings attached to his head in addition" (115).[7]

In her book on Nietzsche's "animal philosophy," Vanessa Lemm (2009) essentially identifies this centaur as a meta-hybrid: a centaur with wings and thus divided three ways by animal, human, and angel. For Lemm, "what distinguishes the virtue of the Centaur (Chiron) is his tactile sensibility. His hands *(chira)* master the art of grasping the occasion *(kairos)*, the instant when animality comes forward through this encounter. The tactile sensibility of the genius of culture is reflected in the terms Nietzsche uses to describe his skills: he uses 'tools' *(Werkzeuge)* and 'manipulates' *(handhabt)* his virtues" (27). Chiron, the most celebrated of centaurs, is thus a creaturely technician, skilled in the arts of medicine as well as music, hunting, and astrological projections.[8] The centaur is thus a figure that helps us explore the sly existence, dormant power, and erotic *technē* of what I would like to call "creaturely love," that is, the nonhuman, ahuman, more-or-less-than-human passion or affect that attracts us to the other in a register beyond or outside the conventional discourse of soul mates.

Hence the fascination afforded by the photograph of Nietzsche and Rée, literally harnessed to Salomé and her utopian vision of a sexually charged, but physically innocent, *ménage à trois*. This awkward image makes explicit the creatureliness that informs *all* our loves and the various bestiaries that give them metaphoric wing (and not only metaphoric). For instance, soon after the studio photo, on July 2, Nietzsche wrote to Salomé, "I wanted to live alone—But the dear bird Lou crossed my path and I believed it was an eagle. And now I wanted the eagle to stay close to me" (in Dufourmantelle 2007, 92).[9] This, not long after writing to her, "I want to be lonely no longer, but to learn again to be a human being. Ah, here I have practically everything to learn!"[10] Like the centaur, Nietzsche considers himself caught between natures—the human and the animal—neither fully one nor the other but pulled in both directions (as if they are mutually exclusive).

For her part, Nietzsche's infamously possessive and manipulative sister, Elisabeth, painted the seductive Russian woman in creaturely terms. In a letter to her friend Carla, also in the same year as the photograph, Elisabeth writes, "How can one call honest that girl who threw herself on Fritz like a wild beast, shredding his good reputation?" And then in her personal diary: "[Salomé has] the character of a cat—a beast of prey that pretends to be a pet . . . a cruelly closed sensuality [and] . . . crude in questions of honor." Two years later, after his sister encouraged a breach with the other two members of the fleeting love triangle, Nietzsche would express regret at having listened to his sister's slanderous taxonomy of his friends, describing her in turn, in a letter to an acquaintance, as "a vengeful anti-Semitic goose" (in Dufourmantelle 2007, 95).

Such totemic descriptions serve to do more than create poetic or malicious analogies. They acknowledge the creaturely continuum we inhabit on a very material and actual register with other life-forms.[11] And while the cultural codings we bestow on animals, and burden them with, may not conform to some actually existing nature or set of values, they *do* help to democratize the human exceptionalism of the Great Chain of Being (which somehow stubbornly survives the trauma of Darwinian understanding).

Rée was the dark horse in all this: the melancholic poet who would never leave the house without a vial of poison in his waist jacket pocket, just in case the world cornered him in an intolerable fashion. He loved Salomé with a semirequited passion, miserably willing to be the third wheel, at least at the beginning, rather than be exiled from her captivating company. She certainly loved Rée enough to make his intimate presence a condition of marrying her husband, Friedrich Carl Andreas (but not enough to satisfy or prioritize him, as she would for another poet, Rilke, later in life). In a letter to Rée, Salomé (1990, 50) wrote, "It's strange, but our conversations have led us automatically toward those chasms, those dizzying places, where one once climbed alone to gaze into the abyss. We've constantly chosen to be mountain goats, and if anyone had heard us, he would have thought two devils were conversing." Finally, after the jealousy which was his daily oxygen became too much, Rée fled Salomé's orbit, leaving behind a letter pleading with her not to come looking for him. Like a wrong-footed mountain goat, Rée died several years later, falling off a cliff while hiking.

Salomé, who appears fatalistic and pragmatic in her memoirs, turns her attentions to her husband, now released from the burden of having to share his free-spirited partner with another man. One of their first discovered affinities is an appreciation of animality. "There was one area in which we were quickly in agreement," she writes in hindsight, "which opened the same doors to both of us: the *world of animals*. This world of the not-yet-human, which so profoundly reminds us of what lies beneath our own humanity, of a simpler and less complicated life no longer in our reach. Our attitude toward individual *animals* was as similar as our attitude toward individual *people* was usually different" (1990, 128). She goes on to note,

A small episode from the early years of our marriage [which] seemed to me characteristic: we had purchased a huge Newfoundland as a watchdog, and one summer night my husband slipped through the garden into the hall to see whether the dog would sense it was his master or think he was a burglar, since he was naked, an unfamiliar state as far as the dog was concerned. Andreas, however, moving with stealth and care, his face a study in concentration, so resembled a stalking predator that—it's hard to put it into words—they were as alike as two mysteries. He became so wrapped up in the inner drama of the animal, in the question of "for" or "against," that he apparently wasn't playing anymore, but seemed to have surrendered to his own twofold wish: for indeed he always wanted new companions to both love and protect him. The dog, in a state of extreme tension, came out of the whole affair with flying colors by reacting to both needs: he *growled* threateningly, but *backed up*. My husband, pleased as could be, laughed aloud, whereupon the dog leaped up to his shoulders and received a joyful hug. (121)

"It is revealing, however," she concludes a few pages on, "that these imprecise comparisons are instinctively drawn from the realm of creatures. One realizes the limited nature of all human measure" (125).[12]

But consistent with her profound hunger for access to Being in its most heightened, sensitive, self-conscious, and articulate state, Salomé would court other, less domesticated creatures, including one of the foremost poets of creaturely life, Rainer Maria Rilke.[13] Reflecting on the passions as she sees them, Salomé wrote, "The perfect gift of an eroticism without inner contradictions is granted only to the animals. In place of the human tension between loving and not loving, they alone know that inner regularity which expresses itself in heat and freedom in a purely natural manner. We alone can be unfaithful" (17–18). This theme of human alienation is consistent with a woman married more to psychoanalysis than to her own husband and with a Western tradition of considering animals as poor-in-world (and thus rich in immediate experience).

Despite Salomé being fifteen years older than Rilke, when they consummated matters in 1897, they were both equally green in matters of the flesh. And given their mutual search for meaning in the midst of fin-de-siècle disorientation, this relationship ran up and down the scale both linking and separating the animal, human, and angel—as well as along the keyboard where the physical and metaphysical touch without blending. Together they made a spiritual pilgrimage to her homeland of Russia, where they paid their respects to Tolstoy and seemed to find a connection to the organic continuum of history that had eluded them in the more modern Western countries of Europe. This rather utopian journey found its emblem in yet another horse, this one just liberated from its cart, returning joyfully to its nightly herd. (An image Rilke would later link to Orpheus in Sonnet XX.) This jointly "witnessed myth" (Andreas-Salomé 1990, 202–3) of their unofficial honeymoon would return to him in an altered form much later, at the side of one Katharina Kippenberg, who also spied a white horse running through a meadow from a train window. Of this moment she wrote, "Rilke and I were both engrossed in contemplation of this horse. 'Now he's going to leap up and gallop off!' I shouted. To my astonishment, I saw the blood rush to Rilke's face. It was flushed so darkly it seemed it would never fade. As though deeply moved, he sat there silently, looking downward, and gave no reply" (203).[14]

For Rilke, this horse seemed to represent a passion that ended when Lou wished to banish him from her life, at the dawn of the new century. ("To make Rainer go away, *go completely away,* I would be capable of brutality. (*He must go!*")) [in Silverman 2009, 88].) Nevertheless, they rekindled their correspondence. And in 1922, more than two decades after their initial affair, Rilke summoned the original equine ghost in a letter to Salomé, soon after completing the tenth and last *Duino* elegy: "I wrote, created the horse. You know, the free happy gray horse with the wooden peg in his foot that once toward evening came upon us in a gallop on the Volga meadow—What is time? When is the present? He leapt over so many years into the wide open spaces of feeling. . . . I went out and stroked little Muzot [the castle where he had been living and writing] that has protected me and ultimately preserved me for so long, as if it were a great old animal" (Andreas-Salomé 2003, 105).[15]

# 3 GROPING FOR AN OPENING

*Rilke between Animal and Angel*

Rilke's poetry was part of a sustained attempt by the author to understand what he called the "Open"—the free, actual, immediate, immanent stream of Being unhindered and unfiltered by human self-consciousness.[1] Rilke's Open occurs outside the walls of the prison house of language—outside the "interpreted world"—and represents a type of unimaginable freedom of access and action, unshackled by second-guessing, interpretation, anticipation, desires, and other human burdens:[2]

> With all its eyes the natural world looks out
> into the Open. Only *our* eyes are turned
> backward, and surround plant, animal, child
> like traps, as they emerge into their freedom.
> We know what is really out there only from
> the animal's gaze; for we take the very young
> child and force it around, so that it sees
> objects—not the Open, which is so
> deep in animals' faces. (2009, 49)

There is, however, one event or exception that can help our finite and fallen selves glimpse the Open, if not move gracefully through it, and that is the epiphanic shock of love. The only problem is that the beloved is *blocking the view*. The emotional and intellectual state of exception that love denotes threatens an ontological shift whereby the cultural blinkers threaten to fall away. The human erotic apparatus, however—and its attendant projections—sabotage the possibility of existential liberty. With the lover's face acting as screen (yes, "in both senses," as media scholars like to say), we dwell together in Plato's cave, ignorant of the exit:

As if by some mistake, it opens for them
behind each other . . . But neither can move past
the other, and it changes back to World. (49)

Given Rilke's yearning for this creaturely experience of continuity, nestled in the womb of everything, the Open—balanced by his skepticism concerning the possibility of access to such a harmonious state of atemporal bliss for our own species—one wonders why he considers his great passion with Salomé to link him to the human. ("Why then still insist on being human," he himself asks in the Ninth Elegy.) Doesn't such an intersubjective connection merely take the lover further away from the pure unthinking ecstasy of the lark and the tiger, the gnat and the bat? According to Salomé's romantic perspective, the poet constantly strives to realize the "peace of the animals and the safety of the angels" (Andreas-Salomé 2003, 20).[3] This is consistent with the dominant gnostic-romantic interpretation of humanity as liminal and exceptional: neither terrestrial nor ethereal but a confused and messy hybrid of both.

Like Nietzsche before him, Rilke saw in "his" Lulu a portal to his own species-being, from which he felt exiled. An instance of this piece of "cruel optimism"[4] is inscribed in a letter dated January 6, 1913, where the poet confesses that it was through Salomé that he felt "linked to the human" (Silverman 2009, 26). What was it about this woman—and this period in intellectual history—that had such giants of the inkpot fretting about their status as human beings and desperately cleaving to her as the medium to achieve it? Just as Nietzsche wanted to be a flogged horse in her company, and the camera lens to capture his "visionary" *jouissance* and abjection, Rilke emphasized his own animality, his own creaturely love, for Salomé. "So now your old mole has once again burrowed a trench for you and cast dark soil right across a perfectly good road" (Andreas-Salomé 2003, 84). When viewed from the perspective of modern animal totems or zoopoetics, Rilke's angels seem more and more like a disavowal of his own—and indeed all humanity's—creaturely loves. Terrible and terrifying as they are, the agonizing proximity and enigmatic intelligence of the angels provide a transcendent security zone from the materialist Darwinian legacy of our fleshly fates and desires.[5] Their very existence, even if only inside the pen and on the page, bears witness to a more-than-creaturely fate. At least that is what Rilke both hoped and felt.

Back on earth, however, the centaur makes a suitably fleeting appearance, not explicitly trapped in the stanzas of the *Duino* poems but roaming freely in the margins of the Second Elegy in particular. Here the narrator asserts,

> If only we too could discover a pure, contained,
> human place, our own strip of fruit-bearing soil
> between river and rock. (2009, 15)

At least one critic has explicitly tied not only this desire but also this topography ("between river and rock") to the figure of the centaur, since between compositions, Rilke was busily engaged in translating a poem by Maurice de Guérin simply called "Le Centaur" (Ryan 1999, 119–20). In this short work, the eponymous creature spies a human walking through a valley usually unsullied by this particular species. The sight of the human shocks and saddens the centaur, because "he was the first [man] my eyes had chanced upon; I despised him. 'There at most,' said I, 'is but the half of me! How short his steps are, and how uneasy his gait! His eyes seem to measure space with sadness. Doubtless it is some centaur, degraded by the gods, one whom they have reduced to dragging himself along like that'" (Guérin 1899, 9). Similar to Nietzsche's vision of the human as an insane, melancholy, *embarrassing* animal, Rilke looks obliquely to the centaur as a more-than-human figure to better outline our mortal failings and foreclosures. And yet, this once-proud narrator has made the fall into old age and the gloom the passing of time can bring in its wake. Centaurs, after all, are not angels. They do not enjoy eternal life. Where once this particular fellow galloped through the fields, at one with the elements, he now suffers the same regrets, and entropic emotions, as we humans are apt to do (at least that is what Guérin's poem suggests). A creaturely kinship is revealed after all, through the winding down of vitality, physicality, and the bone-deep understanding of finitude.

Lulu was clearly attracted to centaurs, given that both Nietzsche and Rilke identified with this figure, at least for a time. We can speculate that they did so, because the centaur is an ideal—albeit paradoxical—figure, representing humanity living in harmony with its animal side. But such reconciliation comes at a cost, as all forms of self-consciousness ultimately seem to do: the cost of nostalgia, of witnessing one's own letting go of the world. Perhaps this is why Rilke, in a letter to Princess Marie von Thurn und Taxis-Hohenlohe (dated May 16, 1911), went so far as to express an only slightly ironic fear of walking in the woods around his present home, lest he encounter "a dried up little centaur" in his path: an experience, no doubt, that would have unpleasantly reminded Rilke of his own attacks of mourning and melancholia (Greene 1969, 26–27).

Better to have one's path crossed by a simple beast, like the unassuming horse or cow—both creatures which would not presume, like the centaur, to speak back in one's own language, thereby disturbing the reassuring (but in fact elaborately constructed) ontological moat between animal and human.

Many summers after the rather grotesque novelty photograph was taken of the odd trio in Lucerne, the older and wiser Salomé decamped yet again to the Alps with her new young lover:

> Rilke . . . and I began to look for a place in the nearby mountains. Having moved out to Wolfratshausen, we changed our little house again. . . . For our second place we were given the rooms over a cowshed at a farmstead built against the side of a hill. The cow was supposed to appear in the photo we took later—she didn't look out the window of the shed. (Andreas-Salomé 1990, 68)

This camera-shy cow, who declined to be photographed, would, we can safely say, be of absolutely no interest to cultural historians, biographers, literary critics, or media theorists. And yet the consistent and sometimes obsessive ways in which this bohemian group of intellectuals and artists viewed themselves through the prism of the animal eye—as much as via the camera eye—suggests that such an absence or refusal on behalf of the cow is significant. (After all, Salomé thought the animal's perhaps willful absence notable enough to mention in her memoirs.)

Despite the relentless emphasis on the human element in matters of the heart, there was in this group, and this time, a partially conscious acknowledgment of the creaturely source of such intense and disorienting passions: that not only do animals herald and witness human affections but these same affects between people are always already (and utterly) *a love between animals.* Rilke's concern for the soul, trapped and abused by the body, may not have been so tortured if he had only followed his creaturely instincts all the way back to the immanence of the Open. Rather than focus on the assumed metaphysical surplus of the linguistic animal, he may have found the freedom he was so desperately looking for in everything from the graceful leap of the gazelle to the indifferent apathy of the cow in his quarters:

> That is what fate means: to be opposite,
> to be opposite and nothing else, forever. (2009, 51)

# 4 ELECTRIC CARESSES

*Rilke, Balthus, and Mitsou*

Rilke had a keen eye for creaturely affection in others as well. In 1920, as Europe reeled from the Great War, as well as from all the questions about human nature and progress that it provoked, the poet visited a close friend, Elizabeth Klossowska, near Lake Geneva. This woman had an eleven-year-old son, who would grow up to be known simply as Balthus, a painter notorious for his voyeuristic depictions of tender-aged girls, often shown in secret, somber interactions with cats. The critical reflex, when confronted with such imagery, was—and indeed still is—to acknowledge the totemic function of this animal within the frame, which symbolically mirrors the girls themselves (coded as feline, or "kittenish"), while also evoking in plain sight a metaphoric allusion to the taboo part of the subject's body he presumably most desired. But this view changes when we learn about a trauma Balthus suffered a year before Rilke's visit.

Having taken in a stray tomcat, the young boy named his new companion Mitsou and loved his enigmatic adoptee with the unthinking intensity of a sensitive child. But just as quickly as it came into his life, the cat disappeared, leaving only a year of memories for the boy to absorb. To cope with the pain of abandonment, the devastated but precocious Balthus made forty ink drawings of fond moments they spent together. Mitsou taken to the park. Mitsou keeping the young boy company as he reads a book. Mitsou in Balthus's arms as they take a lake ferry in summer. Mitsou being scolded after the first dress rehearsal for disappearance. Indeed, the last two pictures in the series show a frantic and disconsolate self-portrait: the young boy searching for his friend and finally crying distraught, showing his empty hands to the viewer.

When Rilke visited the house, one year after this sad event, he was shown the drawings by the budding artist. The poet was so impressed with the story these told that he arranged for the drawings to be published, even writing a short preface in French for the project. Clearly more than sentimental juvenilia—the celebrated German publisher Kurt Wolff, for instance, called them "astounding and almost frightening"—these pictures shed a different light on Balthus's later work, which many find uncomfortably pedophilic. (It is no coincidence that one of his paintings, *Jeune Fille au Chat,* became a cover image for modern editions of Nabokov's *Lolita.*) But, as one recent art critic notes, in the light of these drawings, "Mitsou almost feels like a lost first love."

But why *almost*? Childhood pets allow an experience of intersubjective intimacy too often cast as merely a passing apprenticeship on the long and winding road to proper mature and human love, as if the affection one can have for a cat, dog, or horse is less meaningful or affectively charged as that for a sibling or friend.[1] What Balthus's adult paintings allow, beyond or within the problematic gendered gaze, is the *refusal to choose* between humans or animals when it comes to a privileged object of affection. Or better, it allows us to see a certain continuum between them, of humans *and* other animals, united in play, in boredom, in domestic daydreams.

Rilke's preface, however, reminds us not to collapse such a continuum too quickly. He begins by asking, "Does anyone know cats? . . . I must admit I have always considered that their existence was never anything but shakily hypothetical." Dogs, in sharp contrast, are much easier to "know," since they "live at the very limits of their nature, constantly—through the humanness of their gaze, their nostalgic nuzzlings."

> But what attitude do cats adopt? Cats are just that: cats. And their world is utterly, through and through, a cat's world. You think they look at us? Has anyone ever truly known whether or not they deign to register for one instant on the sunken surface of their retina our trifling forms? As they stare at us they might merely be eliminating us magically from their gaze, eternally replete. True, some of us indulge our susceptibility to their wheedling and electric caresses. But let such persons remember the strange, brusque, and offhand way in which their favorite animal frequently cuts short the effusions they had fondly imagined to be reciprocal. . . . Has man ever been their coeval? I doubt it. And I can assure you that sometimes, in the twilight, the cat next door pounces across and through my body, either unaware of me or as demonstration to some eerie spectator that I really don't exist. (9–10)

In other words, different creatures can inhabit the same objective space (if today's quantum physicists will allow such a conceit), but not the same phenomenological one. Or to paraphrase Lacan, *il n'y a pas de rapport félin*. Cat fur may rub along a human leg, but the cat and the human thus become the locus for two different and unconnected relationships to the same physical contact. There is nothing we could describe as a shared experience. (Of course, the same can be said of human lovers.)[2]

Balthus's own paintings, however, seem to allow for a space of ontological exchange, or at least a possibility of mutual recognition. In one sense, cats are his royal subjects, as in the large canvas *A Portrait of H. M. the King of Cats, Painted by Himself* (1935). In other depictions, the cat has its own sovereign presence and energy, as with *Cat of the Mediterranean* (1949), which served as a mural in La Méditeranée restaurant, in the Place de l'Odéon (an establishment frequented by Malraux, Camus, and Bataille). Clearly Mitsou's soft and elusive fur lived on in many different avatars, produced by the horsetail brushes of his brief "owner." Art thus fulfills one of its primary functions in fixing, or at least attempting to fix, the evanescent essence of the beloved other, the silhouette of another ensouled body that is imminently, if not already, absent.

At the end of his preface, Rilke reflects on the melancholic dynamic of unexpected acquisition and loss, bestowing a special role on cats in the ongoing *fort/da* game that punctuates all our lives (and this sequence is so well phrased and underread that I will succumb to the temptation to quote in full):

> It is always diverting to find something: a moment before, and it was not yet there. But to find a cat: that is unheard of! For you must agree with me that a cat does not become an integral part of our lives, not like, for example, some toy might be: even though it belongs to us now, it remains somehow apart, outside, and thus we always have:
>
> life + a cat,
>
> which, I can assure you, adds up to an incalculable sum.
>
> It is sad to lose something. We imagine that it may be suffering, that it may have hurt itself somehow, that it will end up in utter misery. But to lose a cat: no! that is unheard of. No one has ever lost a cat. Can one lose a cat, a living thing, a living being, a life? But losing something living is death!
>
> Very well, it is death.
>
> Finding. Losing. Have you really thought what loss is? It is simply the negation of that generous moment that had replied to an expectation

you yourself had never sensed or suspected. For between that moment and that loss there is always something that we call—the word is clumsy enough, I admit—possession.

Now, loss, cruel as it may be, cannot prevail over possession; it can, if you like, terminate it; it affirms it; in the end it is like a second acquisition, but this time totally interiorized, in another way intense.

Of course, you felt this, Baltusz. No longer able to see Mitsou, you bent your efforts to seeing her even more clearly.

Is she still alive? She lives within you, and her insouciant kitten's frolics that once diverted you now compel you: you fulfilled your obligation through your painstaking melancholy.

And so, a year later, I discovered you grown taller, consoled.

Nevertheless, for those who will always see you bathed in tears at the end of your book I composed the first—somewhat whimsical—part of this preface. Just to be able to say at the end: "Don't worry: I am. Baltusz exists. Our world is sound.

There are no cats." (12–13)

# 5  BETWEEN PERFECTION AND TEMPTATION

*Musil, Claudine, and Veronica*

Robert Musil, whom the literary critic Frank Kermode described as "a prose Rilke,"[1] went further still in using his own medium as a site of experimentation for considering love's disavowed creaturely aspect. Two early short stories in particular, "The Perfecting of a Love" (Musil 1999b) and "The Temptations of Quiet Veronica" (Musil 1999c), strongly suggest that human sexuality is but a heartbeat away from a bestial passion. Of course, "unbridled" lust has been figured as animalistic since the inception of that long Western tradition concerned with measuring the distance between Man and Beast. The appetites of the body, even before the invention of the Christian soul, have been condemned or belittled as shameful, primitive, or inhuman. And yet Musil complicates the reductive dichotomy of animal–body versus human–soul by evoking complex mental and affective states in which the nonhuman breathes life into the mind as much as the flesh. This refusal, in that radically disoriented age of the early twentieth century, to endorse clear distinctions reaches a vertiginous state of emotional entropy in Musil's modernist sensitivity, as embodied in these sketches toward his epic, but still unfinished, magnum opus *The Man without Qualities*.

Almost plotless, these two long stories (or short novellas) were originally combined under the perhaps ironic title *Unions* (*Vereinigungen*, 1911). Taken together, or on their own, these texts attempt to give voice to the complex, silent, and inherently gendered monologues that inspire or forbid erotic encounters. Indeed, it would be a lifelong struggle for Musil to find the right literary form for his particular hybrid approach to writing: equal parts philosophical speculation and realist fiction. The results are not unlike an erotic phenomenology of the passions, but one that constantly threatens to swallow or shatter the subject of experience. Thus

Musil's pen played the role of wavering needle, fastened to Europe's lost moral compass—nuanced and perceptive, yet also elusive and opaque. From one angle, these stories banish any and all remnants of Victorian sincerity or sentiment. Shift the linguistic kaleidoscope a little, however, and these psychosocial legacies return on a more profound level and in a more modern (i.e., insecure, yet ambitious) guise. We might think of Musil, then, as the poet laureate of ambivalence.

In "The Perfecting of a Love," Claudine, a woman in her thirties, deeply and truly in love with her husband, nevertheless submits to a one-night stand while traveling to her daughter's boarding school. She does not "have eyes" for anyone else, and yet the sheer random and banal nature of the encounter provokes her not only to "betray" the man she adores but to consider the act as a perverse consecration of her wedding vows. Indeed, it speaks to Musil's provocative talents as a writer and thinker that he can render such an amoral scenario as almost a sound piece of logic.[2] The man who seduces Claudine—if we can use such a verb, when the "seduced" is so hyperaware of the seducer's intentions that she yields more out of clinical curiosity than ravished passion—is figured as bestial, in contrast to her husband.[3] This is done with repeated references to his beard, his hirsute physicality, and his clumsy, heavy presence. The animal attraction to this man is pushed to the point of the literal, prompting one critic to state, "Claudine seems to long for pain as part of the pleasure her animal body demands from her. Certainly pure bestiality underlies her attraction to the seducer" (Thiher 2009, 89).

At first, Claudine watches the stranger, whom she meets on a train, indifferently. Even when a snowstorm forces an unscheduled stop overnight in a hotel, she is not at all thrilled by the possibilities: at least, not due to any kind of attraction that he himself embodies in a positive sense. After all, "he might have been anyone; he was no more than a sombre bulk of alien being" (141). And yet, this man's "whomeverness" is what also begins to stir her libido, along with the creatureliness that underscores his impersonality.[4] Slowly, and with a self-conscious and distasteful sense of inevitability, Claudine begins to contemplate responding bodily to his clichéd script. "It was all a matter of an instant. Darkly she sensed that she put her naked feet to the ground like an animal" (144–45). Listening intently to the creaking floorboards outside her bedroom door, "she felt a wave of sudden unreal heat and she almost began to scream, faintly, the way cats sometimes scream in fear and desire, as she stood there, wide awake in the night" (145). Indeed, "all she could feel was the warily prowling, beast-like tread of her own thoughts" (146). At this point, Claudine

> realised obscurely that it was not the stranger who tempted her, but simply this standing and waiting, a fine-toothed, savage, abandoned ecstasy in being herself, *in* being alive, awake here among these lifeless objects— ecstasy that had opened like a wound. And while she felt her heart beating, like some frenzied wild creature trapped within her breast, her body in its quiet swaying drew itself up, like a great exotic, nodding flower that suddenly shudders with the infinitely expanding rapture of mysterious union as it closes round its captive. (146–47)

Musil here, wading deep into a projected stream of consciousness, is working against the generalized amnesia of existence that Heidegger would later diagnose as the forgetting of Being. For the former, literature can be fashioned to attempt an elaborate *remembering* of Being (with all the bodily gestures inscribed in the word). To more fully register the ontological weight or import of any given moment, Musil finds it necessary to undertake an intensive, albeit ultimately inconclusive interrogation of all the disconnects, slippages, and overlaps between psychic, affective, bodily, and social life. We might say, then, that Musil's project is about transindividuation, if we are to use Simondon's language, whereby the human subject emerges within the cracks of contingency, actuality, and the incessant self-narration of identity. As a result of the protagonist's recognition of the generic nature of experience, she appears something like a puppet, haunted by intelligence (itself a decent definition of human being)[5]—a puppet whose intelligence paradoxically prompts automatic behaviors.

This woman, poised on the cusp of considering infidelity as the shortest path toward marital communion, is—in her equivocal fevers—obliged to inhabit the same space that links "human potential" and "human ecstasy" with creaturely desires, instincts, and aversions. For instance, before succumbing to the carnal momentum of the detour, Claudine visits her child's teachers at a boarding school. Even these pedantic and doddering middle-aged men emanate a certain extrahuman musk: "She realised that this was caused by the expression of their faces, which the half-light enhanced by the dull commonness in them that was incomprehensibly transformed by their very ugliness, by a whiff of rutting-time, of enormous, clumsy, troglodyte beasts, that hung about them like an aura" (152). Like her would-be lover, the professors are "too close, too big, like a shaggy animal that gave off an overpowering smell" (154). Nevertheless, she manages to smile, and make small talk, despite being "separated from them only by a deciduous husk, the fabric of chance and actuality" (156).

Creaturely love, as Musil renders it, has an ambient quality—its own libidinal ecology. This is why the affective climate of a mind is prone to the tides of the body. ("And it seemed to her she could understand the way the animals loved, and the clouds, and the sounds in the air.") While there *is* an evolutionary imperative buried deep in sexual antagonisms and attractions, human Eros is not so much about procreation as it is about generic intensities (or what Leo Bersani would call "impersonal intimacy" [Bersani and Phillips 2008])—"the arbitrariness of it, this sense of something very intimate and yet accidental" (158). In the midst of the indiscretion, "a person that she called herself and who was nevertheless not different from everyone else" feels very sorry for herself. "Everything turned into a rocking sing-song of grief at the thought that all this could really happen" (163). Not unlike the far more didactic D. H. Lawrence, taboo sexual practices lurk in the wings of the story, testing the boundaries of what people can do with, and to, each other's bodies and still confidently consider themselves human beings. "Something in her shuddered, something warned her. Sodomy, she thought. That is what it would amount to. But behind that there lay her love's ordeal: 'So that in the realm of reality you shall feel it is I . . . I . . . here under this beast! The unimaginable thing!" And so, while "her body was trembling like an animal hunted down, deep in the forest," she almost sleepwalks into "a state that was like giving herself to everyone and yet belonging only to the one beloved" (176–77).

The interpersonal structure of the other story in the collection, "The Temptations of Quiet Veronica," is similarly triadic, although in this case the two men—the timid Johannes and the more vital Demeter—live in closer quarters with the woman of the title and endure each other's company on occasion. In this plotless but fascinating tale, human sexuality is omnipresent yet opaque, solicitous yet inaccessible. What is more, the traditional "structuring absence" of *literal* creaturely love is not as absent as one would expect, as Veronica is revealed to suffer taboo thoughts about her canine companions (something that would shock most readers even today, with the exception of Donna Haraway [2008]). Thus the animal aspect of human sexuality is not merely subtextual but part of a troubled dialectic between the soil and the soul, the beast and the angel, because for the both author and protagonist, the animal is—unexpectedly— equated with the priest. As Veronica says to her suitor Johannes, not without malice, "Why didn't you become a priest? In a priest there *is* something of an animal! There's that emptiness at the point where other people possess themselves. That meekness—their very clothes reek of it" (185).

In his diaries, Musil explicitly creates this correspondence between priests and animals, signaling the relation between the two in a manner anticipating Kaja Silverman's (2009) sense of *analogy*: going beyond mere likeness to a profound and actual kinship. In this strong definition of the term, a priest is not only "like" an animal but shares an ontological characteristic, which itself creates a meaningful resonance between them—something that demands, or at least *seeks*, recognition or witness. For Silverman, "desire works through analogy" (36), which is "the correspondence of two or more things *with* each other"—rather than *to* each other—"and structures every aspect of Being" (40).[6] So to say, "we *all* 'live through more than we are'" (45).[7] As with the concept of "creaturely love" itself, analogy actively exposes a kinship more profound than similarity, on the level of a coexistence, the consequences of which have yet to be acknowledged or acted upon. The common analogy of animality—where human X is "like" creature Y, or vice versa—has the potential at least to render the two elements an existential anagram. As one Musil commentator writes, "God is the master of disjunction and paradox, a personal impersonal being; something so impersonal, Veroni[c]a reasons, could only be an animal, and she begs Johannes to help her understand why her thoughts center upon bestiality" (Thiher 2009, 93).

In a sense, then, Veronica's temptations are also repulsions, since she considers her suitor Johannes to be weak, while her more sullen sexual option, Demeter, presents himself as both an "enemy and tempter." We barely have a sense of these characters' biographies. They are as vaporous as the prose and the lurching thoughts of Veronica herself. The banal diagnosis for this woman would be hysteria. But unlike Freud's patients, the sexualized animal presences in her mind are not the phantasms of father figures, who threaten more than they protect, but something more impersonal, something less willing to stay within the individual spotlight of family melodrama. As Veronica says to Johannes, recalling a moment of violence between the two men, "that time when Demeter struck you. It seemed to me then you were quite impersonal, stripped right down to something naked, warm, and soft" (185). What both tempts and nauseates Veronica is this vertigo on the precipice of her own fragile species-being. She suffers a negative epiphany: "the only thing that matters is that one should be like the act and not like the person enacting it." This leads her to confess, "To me it seems no human being could be so impersonal. . . . Only an animal could. . . . Oh, help me! Why does it always make me think of an animal?" (190).

Creaturely love, for Veronica—as for Claudine—is an event horizon for her own sense of self.[8] She thus locates its uncanny fascination in her two very different suitors in very different ways, while also admitting—with a strange mixture of panic and fatalism—that it also seeps into her own sense of things. The primal scene for her own creaturely desire is traced back to a memory of the family dog. Indeed, it is necessary to quote this lengthy passage in full, given that it is far too allusive and complex to summarize and, moreover, so emblematic of the language involved when one consciously allows the animal into the bedroom:

> [Veronica felt "that touch before."] It was a memory that she all at once recognised, even across that expanse of years: there it was at last, in incoherent fragments, hot, and still alive. In those days, so long ago, she had loved the hair of a big St. Bernard dog, especially the hair in front where the big chest-muscles rose like two hillocks over the curving bones, protruding at every step the dog took. The mass of that thick coat, and the intense golden-brown of it, overwhelmed her; it was like a treasure beyond counting and like some serene infinitude, so that whenever she tried to keep her eyes fixed on one spot her vision blurred. What she felt was no more or less than the strong, simple, inarticulate affection, the tender companionship that a fourteen-year-old girl will feel for a possession whether animate or inanimate; and yet at this point it was sometimes almost like being in a landscape. It was like walking—here were the woods and the meadow, and here the hill and the field, and in the order of it all each thing was no more than as a little stone simply and perfectly locking into a great pattern, though each, when looked at for its own sake, was seen to be terrifyingly complex and pulsating with repressed life, so marvellous that one had to pause in awe as before an animal crouching tense and still, about to spring.
>
> But once, when she was lying beside her dog like that, it struck her: giants must be like this, with mountains and valleys and forests of hair on their chests, and songbirds among the trees in those hairy forests, and tiny lice on the songbirds, and . . . she could not follow the thought any further, but it might go on like that for ever, here too each thing fitting within the other, so tightly fitted into it that the only reason it stayed still, it seemed, was that it was under the pressure of such great and potent order. And secretly she thought: if the giants grew angry, all this would suddenly fly apart

in all directions, screaming, overwhelming one, over-brimming like some terrifying cornucopia . . . and if it were to fall upon her, raging with love, it would be like thundering mountains and roaring trees, and tiny windblown hairs would grow on her body, crawling with tiny insects, and there would be a voice shrieking in ecstasy because of the ineffable wonder of it all, and her breath would be like a multitude of animals enveloping everything, engulfing the world.

And then, when she noticed that her own breathing made her small pointed breasts rise and fall in the same rhythm as the rising and falling of the shaggy chest beside her, suddenly she felt a sharp dismay and held her breath lest something happen, she did not know what. But when she could not maintain the effort any longer and had to let her breath continue to rise and fall that way, as though that other living creature were slowly drawing it out of her, breath after breath, she closed her eyes and returned to thinking of the giants: it was an uneasy procession of images behind her shut eyelids, but now much nearer to her, and warm as though low clouds were passing over her.

And when she opened her eyes again, much later, everything was just as it had been, only that the dog was now standing beside her, looking at her. And now she suddenly became aware of something protruding from under his meerschaum-yellow coat, a pointed thing, red and crooked as though in voluptuous pain, and in the moment when she tried to get up she felt the warm, flickering caress of his tongue on her face. And then she had been so strangely paralysed, as though . . . as though she were an animal herself, and in spite of the ghastly fear that came upon her something in her cringed and was burning hot, as though now, at any moment . . . like the crying of birds and a fluttering of wings in a hedge, and then a quieting down, soft as the sound of feathers sliding upon feathers. (194–96)

Here we find a vivid instance of what hysteria might look like if the concept were invented by Darwin rather than Freud. Erotic awakening emerges from a libidinal ecology rather than a libidinal economy, "perfectly locking into a great pattern." The scale and the perspective of psychoanalysis are radically altered, so that the ego is coextensive with the environment. Veronica thus oscillates between borderless narcissism—"her breath would be like a multitude of animals enveloping everything, engulfing the world"—and an emptying out into the world: "a quieting down, soft as the sound of feathers sliding upon feathers."[9]

Johannes and Demeter provoke the same oscillation within Veronica, so that *dog* equates with *man,* which equates back to *dog,* in a tail-chasing circle:

> Can you imagine it? She never had a lover again, only those two big dogs of hers. Of course it's perfectly horrible what they say, but just try to imagine it: those two huge beasts, sometimes standing up on their hind-legs, their teeth bared, insistent, masterful, as though you were just the same as they are—and somehow you are. You're terrified of them, with their hairiness, it's all terror except for a tiny point in you where you're still yourself. Yet you know—it needs no more than a single gesture and it'll all be gone in a flash, they'll be servile, they'll crouch, they'll just be animals again. So it's not just animals: this thing is yourself and a solitude, it's you and once again you and an empty, hairy room. It's not an animal's desire, but a desire coming from something else that I can't find any name for. And I don't know how it is that I can understand it so well. (186)

Veronica fears playing the role of a water bowl for a thirsty dog—being lapped up by hot, meaty, slobbering breath. This fear is contagious, to the extent where Johannes becomes crippled by a creaturely self-consciousness, "as though he might suddenly begin to whimper and run on all fours and sniff at Veronica's hair." At times, Veronica herself is written on the page as more textured and material than most literary characters, who—whatever their trials and tribulations—are assumed by the reader to be human: "her large, voluptuous mouth; her bare arms shadowed with faint, black down" (193). As with Claudine, in Musil's companion story, "something in her [Veronica] bristled, soft and electric as a cat's fur—bristled with antagonism to him. . . . And there was a yearning in her to hold him—a yearning that was like the softness of a broken-shelled snail faintly twitching in its search for another, yearning to stick to it tightly even as it dies" (201–2).

# 6   THE BIOLOGICAL TRAVESTY

Veronica could indeed be a character in Rilke's eighth elegy: a woman who catches a glimpse of the Open which lies beyond human narcissism, but the faces of her would-be lovers keep blocking the view. Only forms of life that are unburdened by souls—or, more accurately, unburdened by the *presumption of possessing a soul*—have the potential to see the world with clarity:

> Children and dead people have no souls. But the soul that living people have is what prevents them from loving, no matter how much they may want to; it is that which, in all love, withholds a residue. Veronica was in this moment aware that the thing that cannot be given away by even the greatest love is the very thing that endues all emotions with direction, steering them away from whatever clings to them with timorous faith, the one thing that endues all emotions with something that is inaccessible to even the most dear beloved: something that is always ready to turn away and leave. It is something that even as it comes towards the beloved will smile and, as though keeping some secret pledge, turn and glance back the other way. But children and dead people are either not yet anything or no longer anything, and so it seems possible to believe that they may yet become everything, or that they have been it; they are like the hollowed-out reality of empty vessels, lending their shape to dreams. Children and dead people have no soul—no soul of such a kind. Nor have animals. To Veronica animals were terrifying, a menace in their ugliness; yet in their eyes there was that pin-bright glint of here and now, the falling droplet of oblivion. (Musil 1999c, 209–10)

Both Veronica and Claudine are characters based on episodes in the life of Musil's wife, Martha Marcovaldi, a charismatic yet shy woman nearly seven years his senior whom Musil loved with a fierce and enduring passion. Martha functioned as the prism for all of Musil's luminous imaginings when it came to the feminine, as if no form of sexual or amorous attraction made sense to him unless it was somehow refracted through her. As she was his almost metaphysical Significant Other, Musil would use his writing as a medium to project himself into the impossible space of her subjectivity, which was—from his perspective at least—forever poised on the limit of the human.

And yet it was his mother who gave Musil the first glimpse of the creaturely love that would haunt his mind and pages until the very end. "I recollect vividly," he wrote in his diary, "[a] memory attached to smell: that of the chinchilla fur that belonged to my mother.[1] A smell like snow in the air mingled with a little camphor. I believe that there is a sexual element in this memory although I cannot call to mind anything at all that might bear on this. According to the nuance of my memory of the fur it must have been some kind of desire" (Musil 1998, 187).[2] We need not go the Freudian route to appreciate how the texture of fur could be such a strong libidinal trigger and to further understand how a fur coat can be at once a sleek symbol of urban sophistication *and* the powerful trace of raw mammalian intimacy.[3] Musil, who refers to himself as "le vivisecteur," thereafter uses his pen to navigate the currents of love, lust, shame, and curiosity that animate his inner life and the strange instinctual-yet-reflective behaviors it produces.

In Musil's philosophy, women are closer than men to the almost mystical state he called *non-ratioid*: "in which the bonds of individuality burst open, the soul breaks loose into undifferentiated feeling and merges with the totality of things."[4] One of the key paradoxes concerning Musil's reading of the world is his highly advanced grasp of the generic nature of being—"the man without qualities"—while also championing the monadic, highly individual purchase on life. Hence his admiration for the non-ratioid: "that of singular facts" (255), pertaining to a solitary psyche. Musil had a great respect for the alien aspect of alterity, while simultaneously using this essential distance between beings as an incentive to hazard points of fleeting intersection in his own fictions. What is more, this alterity extended beyond the traditional gulf that separates human lovers to the ontological moats that usually forbid trespass between species.

Writing in his diary, Musil notes, "I hear you putting on your nightgown. But that is not the end of things by a long way. Again there are a hundred small actions. I know that you are hurrying so evidently all of this is necessary. I understand: we watch the dumb behavior of the animals, astonished how, with creatures that are supposed to have no soul, actions follow, one after the other, from morning till night. This is just the same. You have no consciousness of the countless movements that your hands perform, of all the things that seem necessary to you and that are quite inconsequential. But they jut out prominently into your life. I, as I wait, happen to feel this" (167). Elsewhere Musil creates an analogy between married people and animals, given that both classes understand each other at a glance, from the simplest gesture. Befitting such a nonanthropocentric understanding of love, Musil bestowed an animal totem on his beloved, referring to Martha in life and in print as the Raven (an allusion to her jet-black hair).[5] He hoped to write a narrative of that title, "[the] novel of a child, followed through to womanhood, with all the characteristics that are considered pathogenic and disreputable—who becomes happy" (242).[6]

Another of Musil's many unfinished projects was a satirical science fiction story, *The Planet Ed,* which was to detail the miraculous discovery of an inhabited satellite close to the earth. In his notes for this futuristic fable, Musil asks, in telegraphic fashion, "What if one observes people from the perspective of animal psychology, e.g., that of a dog? On a Sunday evening, for example: they bark, play with balls as a dog does with a stone; they feel they have reached their goal when they have a female with them, and vice versa; they seldom pay particular attention to the breed of the other; eating and drinking are among the most important activities. It is probably possible to transfer the whole of the structure of the animal soul to that of the human being. Study of this possibility on a farm. Or ironic reversal with the effect that, in their life together, the dog has become the human being's teacher" (Musil 1998, 421–22). To this thought experiment, Musil adds a quote from Neville Chamberlain, referring to "men who have been brought up to think and speculate." Such men "do not seem to have any inkling of how exceedingly small is the degree of consciousness and reflection in which the totality of mankind lives, and gets by with really rather well" (Musil 1998, 258).[7] Appended to this dry jibe at the Victorian sense of omniscience is a revealing bibliography for the project:

Carl Vogt, Investigations of Animal-States, 1851
Alfred Müller, Title not given, about the gardener ant
Huber, Nouvelles observations sur les abeilles.
Maeterlinck, La Vie des abeilles
J G Romanes, Essays on Instinct, 1897

Fabre, Souvenirs entomologiques

Wundt, Lectures on the Mind of Humans and Animals

Fritz Schultze, Comparative Theory of Souls 1897

Bethe: Is it proper to assign mental qualities to ants and bees?

Forel, speech on 13.8. 1901, at the Zoologists' Congress in Berlin.

(Ants act with conscious reflection.) (257–58)

These "notes to self" sketched in his diary underscore what is clear in the refined writings: that Musil was especially attuned to the operating procedure of what Agamben has called "the anthropological machine." This cultural–material machine constantly attempts—in thought, word, and deed—to sort the animal from the human: itself an impossible task, given that humans are just another leaf of Linnaeus's taxonomic tree, no matter how many tools they like to wield at the service of arguing the contrary and pruning it into a shape to our liking. As we have already seen, Musil was particularly sensitive to moments when this machine threatens to break down, allowing us to see through our own hubris, narcissism, and sense of exception—to see ourselves as first and foremost kinfolk of the beasts. In a brief diary entry, for instance, Musil writes, "The motion of a woman on a horse has—seen from beneath, from a bench—an immense sensuality about it. As if, with each step, she were being seized from below by a wave and lifted upward" (Musil 1998, 149). We see Musil's expansive anthropology more problematically in the racial coding of his classic Orientalist male gaze: "The negress: I think Somali or Abyssinian. In European dress, shallow bell of velvet, with hair darting out from underneath. Saddle-nose; speaks like a flock of starlings. The inside of the hands light-colored, speckled with pink. Mythical creature. I should like to kiss you under the armpits" (164).

We see this sensibility come into focus also when women are subtracted from the picture:

Here, about four weeks ago, I saw a horse laughing. This was at the Viale della Regina. A small, elegant young carriage-horse. It was tied up to a wall (on the unpaved footpath, to the left, in a gap in the houses, was an "osteria" or a wagoners' workshop, a place with courtyard, bushes, sugarcane) being curry-combed by a groom. The inside of his thighs was his sensitive spot. The closer the man came, the further back it laid its ears, became restless, tried to move its mouth there—which the man prevented with his body— and stepped from one foot to the other. When the man had reached the actual spot the horse couldn't stand it anymore, tried to turn around, to force him away. And because the man was stronger and didn't let it change position it had to stand still but shook over all its body and bared its teeth. Just like a human being who is being tickled so much that he can't laugh any longer. (168)

For Musil, as for many others, animals are "people" too: an ongoing realization that needs to be *re*-realized every day, lest it be erased and effaced by the conscientious workings of the anthropological machine.[8] Hence the diary entries where Musil proposes "the following kinds of experiments: husbands or wives who [only] live as long as dogs or horses. This intense attachment lasting 8 or 14 years. What forms does love take? Or other ones who live as long as trees." Or else where he sketches the outline of a tale which reverses Turgenev's *Fathers and Sons,* in which a young woman accidentally witnesses her new fiancé being seduced by her own mother: "The daughter is taken aback. Up till now she has only known a woman's kiss as a tentative gesture; but this is like a dog sinking his teeth into another—which is something she once saw—or when a lion at a zoo seizes hold of the piece of meat that the keeper holds out to it" (398).

It seems only fitting, then, given this aesthetic compulsion to search for the secret and source of desire beyond our own (human) skin, that Musil's diaries end with a scene of feline sexual congress, only a mile or two from the very spot where Balthus found, and soon lost, his Mitsou. Hiding from the Nazis with his Jewish wife—unwell, unread, and financially insecure—Musil was only too aware of the possible consequences of such systematic dehumanization: itself an ugly symptom of humanity's contempt for animals (genocide being only the most obviously lethal extension or mode of the anthropological machine). Looking out of his window in the fragile haven of Geneva, 1941, Musil certainly felt a great foreboding of the war raging over the mountains. And yet his final recorded observations, before dying of a stroke, were of the local "cat music":

The day before yesterday the cats started a season of love. Because of the position of my room with its big windows I am, so to speak, on the same level as they are. . . .

The beautiful stranger. The surface of her hair has a clear porcelain sheen. Two shades of grey; or white with brown-grey layers; or greenish-brown layers. A charming little nose. A soft, no longer girlish shape; one cannot say that this is "of perfect beauty" since it is, after all, an alien form of beauty for us; one might say, rather, that it is beautiful in its perfection. Everything about her is uniform, slow and supple. Her eyes are of shining green. They are too indifferent to be called "radiant." She is quite large. She has a small head. I do not know who it was who painted women like her. Botticelli, perhaps. She would be in her mid-twenties.

On the first day, a small, dirty, white tomcat paid court to her. He is no youngster. Not strong, but well-made. They met each other time and again as if by chance. If he was not there, she went to look for him. When he came, she sat down unintentionally in his path. He sat down close to her. He made music. He is a courtly singer. She listened attentively to him; but in the fashion of a lady who does not indicate what it is that moves her. She bestowed on him her favor—her attention, that is—and also the friendly desire to share his company. . . . She is not frightened or inhibited when one goes to the window. Looks up, and her gaze is soft and friendly, but unattainable since it comes from another life that now has nothing to do with the life of humans. (500–501)

And yet, a few days later:

We are in Zurich, at the "Fortuna Boarding House." I did not experience the "season of the cats" right through to the end. . . . On the third or fourth day, already, things became rather vulgar. . . . fur flew all around when the magnificent female and the beautiful young tom were rolling about in the grass. Apparently he was trying to roll her onto her back but she was too strong and put up too serious a resistance. They parted in anger. The female then returned to no avail. The next day she came past our door with a remarkable expression as if, in the meantime, far too much had happened to her. She no longer seemed to have stepped from some fairy tale, but had a distracted air about her and also that unwashed appearance that made her look as if she had been on a railway journey.

. . . *The biological travesty, nonetheless very touching, that is love.* . . .

If circumstances prevent coitus (or even coitus interr.) there is a residual need—quite separate from soulful tenderness—to snuggle up close, to touch, to catch hold of some of the softness and warmth. There is something similar to this in the way cats behave when they content themselves with following each other at a distance or sit down five paces apart. This is the first physiological step leading to much that is human. The tender dependence of the child on the mother; its desire to snuggle close and be warm; its happiness when it does so; this non-sexual eros that Freud interprets as sexual. It may be in fact the physical continuation of whatever it is that cannot be finished physically, or of whatever cannot be carried out immediately. (502, emphasis added)

# 7 "THE CREATURE WHOM WE LOVE"

*Proust and Jealousy*

We reach for the word *creature,* in an erotic context, either when we want to slander someone we find repellent or when we want to exult someone we find exceptionally attractive. Any psychoanalyst will attest that such ambivalence is an essential aspect of Eros and that hatred is but the yin for love's yang. But this rather "schizophrenic" usage of our key term is worth noting for other reasons, in that it underscores the radically unstable and unpredictable role that the figure of the creature plays in our little kitchen-sink dramas and bedroom farces. Concerning the latter, Marcel Proust is still perhaps the most perceptive guide, even if the loquacious affectations and refined snobbisms of his native gilded-age Paris now seem a universe away from the swift, mumblecore fumblings of the hookup generation. This, not only because we can easily imagine the Baron de Charlus using Grindr to find young men to please him, but because *The Search* is still the ultimate statement in Western literature detailing the agonistic symbiosis between image and intellect, desire and drive, specter and spectacle (couplets embodied, according to Agamben, in the nymph). For the narrator, Marcel, all these "fugitive creatures" that haunt and tempt him throughout his apprenticeship in the jealous signs and sighs of love are the real-life phantasms that provide the raw material of self-transcendence: what Martha C. Nussbaum (2005) has called "the contemplative ascent."[1] Nevertheless, as Proust (2006, 438) notes, "every impulse of jealousy is individual and bears the imprint of the creature . . . who has aroused it."

Symptomatic, then, is the frequency with which the creature makes an appearance in Proust's universe: from the rhetorical (as when a character is described by another as a "heavenly" creature) to the literal (as when Albertine sleeps under Marcel's gaze and is revealed in all her mysteriously material unhuman attraction).[2] In *Sodom and Gomorrah* alone, we meet a "heavenly creature," "sublime creature," "gorgeous creature," "marvelous creature," "excellent creature," "adorable creature," and "beloved creature." But given the capricious nature of the characters who use such language, we feel that the adjective could change in a heartbeat, at the slightest sign of slight or insult, thus revealing a "loathsome creature." Once again, we detect the unstable nature of the term, eliciting approval and revulsion in equal measure.

Consider this *mise-en-abime* of Proust's entire project:

> They know themselves well enough to have observed that in the presence of the most divergent types of woman they felt the same hopes, the same agonies, invented the same romances, uttered the same words, to have deduced therefore that their sentiments, their actions bear no close and necessary relation to the woman they love, but pass by her, spatter her, surround her, like the waves that break round upon the rocks, and their sense of their own instability increases still further their misgivings that this woman, by whom they would so fain be loved, is not in love with them. Why should chance have brought it about, when she is simply an accident placed so as to catch the ebullience of our desire, that we should ourselves be the object of the desire that is animating her? And so, while we feel the need to pour out before her all those sentiments, so different from the merely human sentiments that our neighbour inspires in us, those so highly specialised sentiments which are a lover's, after we have taken a step forward, in avowing to her whom we love our affection for her, our hopes, overcome at once by the fear of offending her, ashamed too that the speech we have addressed to her was not composed expressly for her, that it has served us already, will serve us again for others, that if she does not love us she cannot understand us and we have spoken in that case with the want of taste, of modesty shewn by the pedant who addresses an ignorant audience in subtle phrases which are not for them, this fear, this shame bring into play the counter-rhythm, the reflux, the need, even by first drawing back, hotly denying the affection we have already confessed, to resume the offensive, and to recapture her esteem, to dominate her; the double rhythm is perceptible in the various periods of a single love affair, in all the corresponding periods of similar love affairs, in all those people whose self-analysis outweighs their self-esteem. (201)

While there is no explicit reference to the creature here, the narrator does explicitly suggest that passionate love is something other than human: "so different from the merely human sentiments that our neighbour inspires in us." Here we see the long shadow of Augustine, in which the narcissism inherent in creaturely love blots out the radiance of the kind we should aspire to: the human love of the neighbor, which functions as the imperfect dress rehearsal for the eternal "indifferent" affection of His Divine Omniscience.[3]

Although society may frown on love affairs conducted between the classes—such as the one between Swann and Odette—it nevertheless tolerates and sometimes even indulges them, provided the couple has the right combination of youth and charm. An affair between people of the same gender, however, is the scandal that animates *Sodom and Gomorrah* as well as Proust's own enterprise (insofar as personal inclination is bound to influence a text—though never in easily translatable ways).[4] In this volume, the old, rich pederast Monsieur Charlus—whose eyes swivel in public, "like a frightened animal"—plays a key role, his barely concealed "inverted" desires reminding us again of the centaur: "In M. de Charlus another creature might indeed have coupled itself with him which made him as different from other men as the horse makes the centaur, this creature might indeed have incorporated itself in the Baron, I had never caught a glimpse of it. Now the abstraction had become materialised, the creature at last discerned had lost its power of remaining invisible, and the transformation of M. de Charlus into a new person was so complete that not only the contrasts of his face, of his voice, but, in retrospect, the very ups and downs of his relations with myself, everything that hitherto had seemed to my mind incoherent, became intelligible" (22).

For the narrator, paranoid about the possibility of being cuckolded by the modern daughters of Sappho ("creatures marvellously inhuman"), there is a certain brutality in homosexuality: a brutality amply incarnated in Charlus's body and behavior, "for every creature follows the line of his own pleasure, and if this creature is not too vicious he will seek it in a sex complementary to his own" (28).[5] The taboo nature of the love that dare not speak its name leads to geometrical perversions, above and beyond the standard moral ones: "every man of the kind of M. de Charlus is an extraordinary creature since, if he does not make concessions to the possibilities of life, he seeks out essentially the love of a man of the other race, that is to say a man who is a lover of women (and incapable consequently of loving him)" (36). But no matter who the love-object is in Proust— whether one's own gender or not—the epithet "creature" signifies a person who does not fully belong in the category of the human: either because of their ethereal beauty or talents or because they do not rise to the civilized criteria of the species. They are either superhuman or subhuman. "Don't you think it criminal," says Mme. Verdurin to the Baron, speaking of the musician Morel, "that that creature who might be enchanting us with his violin should be sitting there at a card-table. When anyone can play the violin like that!" An observation which stands in contrast to the violent objection she makes to another one of her "faithful," Brichot, when confronted by his laundress in his apartment: "What! . . . a woman like myself does you the honour of calling upon you, and you receive a creature like that?" (233).

Indeed, Proust even gives us license to consider sections of his epic search for lost time as variations on the old animal bride story. Marcel's first love, for instance (besides his mother, of course), is Gilberte, who is described in *Within a Budding Grove* as a Melusine: a mermaid-figure who moved between aquatic and terrestrial worlds, thanks to the metamorphoses afforded by marriage (and its dissolution). More explicitly, the domestication of Gilberte's successor, Albertine, in *The Captive* is presented in animalistic terms: "She would never think of shutting a door and, on the other hand, would no more hesitate to enter a room if the door stood open than would a dog or a cat. Her somewhat disturbing charm was, in fact, that of taking the place in the household not so much of a girl as of a domestic animal which comes into a room, goes out, is to be found wherever one does not expect to find it and (in her case) would— bringing me a profound sense of repose—come and lie down on my bed by my side, make a place for herself from which she never stirred, without being in my way as a person would have been" (458). Indeed, it turns out that Albertine is so easily trained that she will only enter the master's room at the sound of a bell! (The irony being that she very well may become a wild minx again, as soon as she escapes the domestic space.)

Jealousy, in Proust, is the most formidable feature of passionate love, with its own urgent temporality, burning within the green flame of the present and yet seeking clues of infidelity in past and future alike. In this sense, it is the shadow of the kind of redemptive compassion, and letting go of the petty injuries of the ego, that the entire *Search,* taken as whole and in retrospect, seeks and encourages. Yet it is "the revolving searchlights of jealousy" that can illuminate the animal aspect most efficiently, whether it be through the horns of cuckoldry or the talons of possessive mania. To take only one example, the gifted violinist mentioned earlier, Morel, works himself into a fury when he has occasion to question the chastity of his fiancée. Marcel witnesses the scene, in which Morel loses all decorum and dignity, calling his bride to be a "dirty slut" on a public street. To the narrator, the scene depicts "the amorous rage of an infuriated animal." Moreover, the attack is "as bestial as the scene to which (minus the words) a woman might be subjected by an orang-outang that was, if one may use the expression, enamored of her" (606). Morel's almost instantaneous regret prompts him to sit on the side of the street and sob, inspiring Marcel to see evolution occur in fast-forward, right there in front of his eyes: "this evening, within a few hours, centuries had elapsed and a new sentiment, a sentiment of shame, regret, grief, showed that an important stage had been reached in the evolution of the beast destined to be transformed into a human being" (606). We suspect it will only take another hesitation or blush to reverse the chronology, and the taxonomic status of the lover.

Certainly it is significant that the narrator considers Albertine—who jumps both into motor cars and onto her lovers "with the light bound of a young animal rather than a girl" (355)—in a very different light when she is fast asleep in his house. While gazing at her full-face, untroubled by an evasive or returning gaze, Marcel is finally able to find relief from the horns that forever threaten to sprout painfully from his forehead. "My jealousy grew calm, for I felt that Albertine had become a creature that breathes, that is nothing else besides" (540)—suggesting that it is the so-called human element that tortures the lover:

> By shutting her eyes, by losing consciousness, Albertine had stripped off, one after another, the different human characters with which she had deceived me ever since the day when I had first made her acquaintance. She was animated now only by the unconscious life of vegetation, of trees, a life more different from my own, more alien, and yet one that belonged more to me. Her personality did not escape at every moment, as when we were talking, by the channels of her unacknowledged thoughts and of her gaze. She had called back into herself everything of her that lay outside, had taken refuge, enclosed, reabsorbed, in her body. In keeping her before my eyes, in my hands, I had that impression of possessing her altogether, which I never had when she was awake. Her life was submitted to me, exhaled towards me its gentle breath. (503)

As Nussbaum (2005, 230) notes (a critic whose name originally means "nut tree"), it is "only when a human being becomes a plant that she can be loved without hatred."

For Swann, whose sufferings on account of jealousy set both stage and tone for those of the narrator, the animal attraction of Odette is so power-ful that it becomes *itself* a creature in Swann's mental life, accompanying him through the nocturnal streets of the city. Swann "would get into his carriage and drive off, but he knew that this thought had jumped in after him and had settled down upon his lap, like a pet animal which he might take everywhere, and keep with him at the dinner-table, unbeknownst to his fellow-guests. He would stroke and fondle it, warm himself with it, and, overcome with a sort of langour, would give way to a slight shuddering which contracted his throat and nostrils" (Proust 1982, 294).[6] Here crea-turely love is a virtual familiar that can keep one company, in anguish as well as anticipation. Ultimately, for Proust, the human and the creatural are inseparably entwined around each other, like DNA coils, because it is impossible to have one without the other. What's more, the beloved is *always already* a creature: of society, certainly, but also overflowing it— escaping our human condescensions, including and especially the weak-ness to extend charity to those we ourselves have exploited in the libidinal economy of sexual commerce. "When we count up afterwards the total amount of all that we have done for a woman," Marcel writes, "we often discover that the actions prompted by the desire to show that we love her, to make her love us, to win her favours, bulk little if any greater than those due to the human need to repair the wrongs that we have done to the creature whom we love, from a mere sense of moral duty, as though we were not in love with her" (Proust 2006, 203).

# 8 THE LOVE TONE
*Capture and Captivation*

In the slavish, almost automatic cleaving to the beloved that is the sign of passionate love, we seem to be "reduced" to an animal state. After all, Heidegger went to great lengths to detail the ways in which the human—and *only* the human—has the potential to awake from evolutionary captivation and go beyond those instinctual triggers (what he calls the "disinhibitors") that mesmerize the biological body and mind. Humans, it is argued, are the only species that can *think* our way out of an instinctive fixation or compulsion, since our capacity for language and rational thought is a magical instrument with which we can sabotage the rather one-track-minded plans of Mother Nature. Which is why the captivated lover is such an embarrassing figure in polite society. He or she (but in Proust, certainly a he) is a troubling reminder that we may at any moment collapse back into the presumed automaticity of the animal. The feverish, darting, and distracted eyes of the lover are the inhuman expression of the cornered beast and of blind evolutionary drive: like the bee that won't stop eating nectar, because its abdomen has been sliced open, or the monkey who becomes trapped, simply because it refuses to let go of the banana in the basket. The lover might even devolve into a ticklike thing: a dormant creature that responds only to one or two types of stimuli and then springs into laser-focused action. The lover is unhuman, because he or she is captivated by his or her own captivity.

Marcel's fraught existence as essentially Albertine's zookeeper obliges us to wonder who is in fact the captive. As with Hegel's master–slave dialectic, the apparent position of subservience holds a good share of the power, according to the logic of recognition, and the need for such in the putative dominant partner. To have one's heart captured by another necessitates a countercapture to ensure an impossible symmetry. But must we flatter our own species-being by condescending to the lover, captivated by the beloved? Must we see subhumanity in a charged state like this?[1] For the pioneering Estonian biologist Jakob von Uexküll, all creatures are ensconced in their own *Umwelt,* or environment, which functions like a bubble, nestled within the wider world. Animals, including humans, have radically different phenomenological experiences by virtue of their very different organs of perception and intervention. Uexküll—recently described as "a kind of biologist-shaman attempting to cross the Rubicon to nonhuman minds" (Dorion Sagan, in Uexküll 2010, 20)—did not presume humans have the most complex or comprehensive access to the wider world, because our stimuli is limited in specific ways. For instance, the human olfactory *Umwelt* is poor-in-world when compared to, say, a dog's. But the essential insight is that the *Umwelt* of any individual—no matter the species—is the direct result of what we can sense, via the various physiological interfaces at our disposal (and the cognitive interpretive systems they in turn create or require). According to such a scheme, the enamored Swann or Marcel, suddenly wracked with jealousy, would be living in a suddenly diminished *Umwelt,* in which he develops the most exquisitely sensitive organs to detect falsehood or evasiveness. At the same time, the rest of the world—anything that doesn't pertain to their love-object—recedes into a vague and gray lo-definition background.[2]

For Uexküll, the animal requires a "perception image" to succeed in the two main tasks of existence: feeding and breeding. To "see" a grasshopper, a jackdaw must already have both a "perception image" and a corresponding "search image" of what a grasshopper looks like. Uexküll's experiments suggested that jackdaws have no perception image of a resting grasshopper and are thus incapable of eating one when the insect is standing stock-still. The stationary grasshopper simply does not exist within the jackdaw's *Umwelt.* Only when the smaller creature moves can the bird recognize its dinner and pounce with its beak. The search image thus corresponds with the perception image, and life springs into action. (Think of how ball boys and ball girls at Wimbledon "become-animal" in their temporary reduction of the search and perception image to a fuzzy yellow ball.)[3] In a section titled "The Companion," Uexküll explicitly links pregiven pattern recognition with the need for companionship: the animal search for a fellow creature to spend time with, beyond the urgency of sustenance and reproduction. The mother-companion, for instance, is a common requirement, and the perception image of an animal may be satisfied with a reasonable approximation. Hence all the online videos of lions raising piglets or puppies being mothered by capybaras.

"The same occurs in the choice of the love companion," explains Uexküll:

> Here, too, the acquired signs of the substitute companion are so surely engraved that an unmistakable perception image of the substitute companion is created—after the first confusion has occurred. As a consequence of this, even animals of the same species are rejected as love companions. This is most clearly illuminated by a delightful experience. In the Amsterdam Zoo, there was a pair of bitterns of which the male had "fallen in love" with the zoo director. In order to allow the bitterns to mate, the director had to stay out of sight for quite some time. This had the positive result that the male bittern became accustomed to the female. This ended up in a happy marriage, and, as the female sat brooding over her eggs, the director dared to show his face once more. And what happened then? When the male saw his former love companion again, he chased the female off of the nest and seemed to signal by repeated bows that the director should take his proper place and carry on the business of incubation. (111–12)

Queer nature indeed!

Clearly Odette, Gilberte, and Albertine function as perception images within "the search image" of Proust's wider search for lost time. They may be practically invisible for the narrator, until such time as they move and correspond to a pregiven fantasy space (compare the girl-gang walking along the sand at Balbec). But once the companion has been established ("chosen" may be giving too much agency), the search image suspends itself, until such time that it is needed again. Uexküll himself refers to the exclusive nature of what he calls "the love tone" (113)—in this case a jackdaw that initiates courting rituals in the presence of a chambermaid—so that all other perception images become "ineffectual."[4]

Love is thus revealed to be a restricted operation of biosemiotics. All well and good. But does this mean that human love is inevitably conducted on the level of the animal? Or might animals be less "animalistic" than we think? For the French philosopher Jean-Christophe Bailly, the animal kingdom is a far more subtle place than we usually suspect, with more room for play and invention within and between the immediate bubbles of our species-centric environments. For Bailly (2011, 53), "sexuality is no more exhausted among animals than it is among human beings in the straight and 'instinctual' line of intercourse." Indeed, "admirable is the extent of invention in the realm, [and] admirable are the solutions that animals have found so that they can go about the world, rub up against the limits of their *Umwelt* and perhaps stretch those limits in the process" (43). Relying on the ancient idea of *psyche*—borrowed from Plotinus, who sees life itself as a living form of thought—Bailly views the psyche as describing "a dimension that oscillates between ritual (the pure and simple execution of a dance) and improvisation (the invention of that dance)" (54). (Consider, for instance, the undecidability between code and improvisation with the courtship rituals of bowerbirds.)

Indeed, it is worth quoting Bailly at some length here:

> Insofar as we can tell by observation, the behavior of desiring animals . . . far from being reduced to pure fascination or stupor, includes complex rituals, elaborate procedures of approach and seduction, and rivalries. From displayed offering, from caress to combat, the amorous drama of animals seems to be woven, like that of humans, out of play and epic scenarios. It behooves us here to be just as suspicious of a sort of triumphal pansexualism as of an anthropomorphic sentimentality eager for pleasant anecdotes that have been accumulating since antiquity. . . .
>
> Now, these activities and everything that forms and informs the *Umwelt* make every animal mode of being a passionate mode, passionately occupied. And if there is indeed a program, as has been claimed over and over, there is also interpretation: the species does not unfold in lock-step, it branches out and disseminates, takes risks; it has its scouts as well as its homebodies. The will to live, of which the search for food and the search for a sexual partner are high points, in fact agitates and troubles every animal: instead of supplying animals with a bundle of ready-made answers, the will to live manifests itself in the form of a constant interrogation, through numerous operations (obstacles to surmount, ruses to refine, channels to reopen, and so on). (53–54)

Between these two passages we see the glow of a dawning appreciation of meta-instinctual animal life, which has yet to extend beyond specialized ethological studies or esoteric ecopoetic accounts. The standard accusation assembled to stifle such talk is usually that of anthropomorphism: the projection of our own presumed freedoms onto the fully captivated, and thus circumscribed, life of the animal. But animals are not algorithmic. Let's not forget that we ourselves emerge from the same terrestrial matrix and are still dominated by the search for food and the search for a sexual partner. Seduction isn't something that only happens in Parisian cafés.

It happens in your back garden or deep below the cold ocean, while you are sleeping soundly in bed—and in more creative and unexpected ways than you might think.[5] (A quick scan of the most recent books on biology will confirm this claim.)[6]

As Bailly insists, "this is how we have to imagine animal life, the lives of animals: living beings immersed in significance, constantly attentive, that have nothing but appearances, perhaps, the always wavering movement of appearances" (55). Moreover, the very self-positing of an "I"—to seduce or be seduced—is not the exclusive right of the human. Derrida calls this emergent, or at least previously unacknowledged, self-awareness of animals *auto-deixis*. The term describes a de facto pointing to the self, *by* the self, by the very same creatures that the Western tradition has considered essentially soulless automatons, in which the light is on but nobody's home. (Signaled by the pronoun we use, where, say, a bird wavers between a *she*, a *he*, and an *it*.) But who can deny, Derrida (2008, 95) asks, "that phenomena of narcissistic exhibition in seduction or sexual combat, the 'follow me who is (following) you' deployed in colors, music, adornments, parades, or erections of all sorts derive from such an auto-deixis?"[7] To get laid, the argument implies—whether an insect or a human being—one must have at least exhibited a rudimentary "auto-referential self-distancing" (94). One must point at the self, in front of the (desired) other, as if to say, "Get a load of this!" In which case, there is an auto-deictic continuum between the peacock strutting around the royal gardens and John Travolta parading down a Queens boulevard to the disco.

There is no "I" in Nature. But then again, there might be. Just a different kind of "I" to the ones we are used to dealing with.

# 9 "THE SOFT WORD THAT COMES DECEIVING"

*Fournival's* Bestiary of Love

Long before the modern explosion of industry and human striving, there were notable attempts to depict the mutual attraction and antagonism of the sexes as if these were in fact a matter of species or *Umwelt* rather than gender. One such text is Richard de Fournival's *Bestiary of Love,* which was written in France in the middle of the thirteenth century and is now considered the first literary endeavor to splice two very different traditions together: bestiary lore and the epistolary romance. Fournival's slim book—split in two parts, with the man addressing his lady, followed by a spirited response—is, therefore, an important contribution to the human understanding of creaturely love and a compressed lesson on the animal origins or implications of what we do in the name of the heart (or, at least, what "we" did in medieval times).

As the modern translator, Jeanette Beer, notes in her introduction, "Richard plays cock, ass, wolf, and cricket, successively, and his beloved is in her turn a wolf, a crow, and a viper" (Fournival 2000, xi). This menagerie parades before the reader to draw attention to certain shared characteristics between lover and animal, once again demonstrating the importance of analogy to self-perception and self-conception. Here the beast in question at any given moment is a measure that collapses the distance it is designed to maintain, so that the female love interest is "like" a snake in certain ways, according to Master Richard, but then again, is not (so far as he needs to point out the resemblance for it to be registered). These analogies are, then, as slippery as the viper she sometimes (almost) becomes.

For Beer, the book is revolutionary for its time in the fact that "the love activities of a man and a woman are by implication assimilable (and often inferior!) to the characteristics of so-called lower animals" (xi). Moreover, love is not necessarily presented as a noble calling but instead is depicted as a crow picking out a man's brain through his eye sockets (the more intelligent the brain, the more vulnerable and tasty the prey). From our millennial perspective, Master Richard's zoological approach to Eros speaks of a conflicted resentment toward the power women hold when they are the object of such heightened fascination. Hence the opening lines, in which the ugly and horrendous voice of the "despairing man" is compared to the braying of a Wild Ass. This state soon morphs into something more akin to the canine: "For if I could have acted like The Dog, which is of such a nature that, after vomiting, it can return to its vomit and re-eat it, I would happily have swallowed down my pleading a hundred times, after it flew out through my teeth" (5).

For her part, according to Master Richard, the woman is like the wolf in three distinct, figurative ways: first, she cannot bend without swiveling her whole body. Second, she only captures her prey a long way from home. And third, she will, so to speak, gnaw on her own body in revenge for stepping on a twig when sneaking up on prey:

> All these natures can be found in woman's love. For she cannot give herself in any way but totally. That conforms with the first nature. In conformity with the second, if it happens that she loves a man, she will love him with the utmost passion when he is far away from her, yet when he is nearby she will never show a visible sign of love. In conformity with the third nature, if she is so precipitate with her words that the man realizes she loves him, she knows how to use words to disguise and undo the fact that she has gone too far, just as the wolf will avenge itself on its foot with its mouth. (6)

But if the woman is, at times, like a wolf—and at others like a viper—then Love itself is an even more ferocious beast: the lion, "for Love attacks no man unless he looks at Love" (9). In an era in which the natural philosophy of Aristotle was still the most rigorous form of early ethology, the line between fable, myth, biology, and behaviorism was very blurry indeed. (At one point, the narrator even refers to the then well-known antipathy between elephant and dragon.) But the lesson to be drawn is not the superstition of the premodern past but rather the persistence with which these allegorical animals continue to inform the way we look at animals (including ourselves).

Love, for the man in this bestiary, is both a terrifying creature and the snare with which we trap our prey. Master Richard makes reference to the Sirens: monstrous avian-women whose inhuman call lures men to their doom. "Was it surprising that I was captured?" he writes. "No, for Voice has so much power that it excuses many things that are unpleasant, as with The Blackbird." Perhaps confused by the intensity of his passion, the man shifts registers and species with a capricious abandon mirroring his target—the fickle female heart. One minute, Master Richard is captured by his own reflection, like a tiger in the mirror (14). The next minute, he is a unicorn, summoned against his will by "the sweet smell of maiden-hood" (15), only to find she is a treacherous decoy. Seized through the five senses—especially hearing, sight, and smell—the male lover is at the mercy of his captor, so that only reciprocation will release him from his wretched bondage. Only a kiss of resuscitation will reverse "the love-death which killed me" (19).

Such emotional blackmail was no doubt as familiar to the maidens of courtly love as it is today to the women of online dating.[1] ("But my lord, pray how doth an electronic response to thy profile oblige me to put thy dragon in my mouth?") For Master Richard, women who claim to love yet "refuse to give themselves" are like the weasel, "which conceives through its ear and gives birth through its mouth." Indeed, he pushes this point as hard as he can: "So fair, very sweet beloved, if my pleading annoys you as much as you say, you might as well deliver yourself from it by giv-ing up your heart, because I am pursuing you only for that. Why would I pursue you if not for that, when nothing else but that can be of any use to rescue me from death by love?" (20–21). Given the veiled and mod-est discourse of the age, it is never entirely clear whether the man in this scenario seeks exclusive romantic attention only, or access to her body. No doubt the early romance genre as a whole—not to mention the read-ers of the time—get their energy from the power of this ambiguity. What does the act of "making love," for example, actually entail when it comes to those swallow-like people who do "nothing except in flight. They even make love only in passing. As long as their love is in sight it has meaning for them, nothing more" (22). We might even go so far as speculate that the origin of the sexual phrase "to get laid" comes from the kind of meta-phors found in Fournival's bestiary, given that "laying and rearing are to be compared with two things that are found in love: capturing and keep-ing. For as the egg is without life when it is laid, and does not live until it is hatched, so the man, when captured by love, is as if dead and he does not live until he is retained as a lover. . . . Since you have laid (that is, cap-tured) me, there is no woman, if she were to hatch (that is, retain) me who would not lose me" (28–29).

Finishing the letter to his lady with a final plea for mercy, Master

Richard begs her not to confuse him with the vulture, who only follows out of habit. But a note of sincere exasperation is struck when he laments, "But I cannot by any power of words make you know the species to which I belong" (36). For the author, Fournival, some satisfaction must have been gleaned from his impressive feat of ventriloquizing the (unnamed) lady herself.

She begins her response with a theological history lesson:

> God who by His dignity and power created the whole world and first made heaven and earth and all that is established in the one and in the other, after ward made man to be the noblest creature He could devise. And it pleased God to make man out of a substance that is not among the most suitable of substances. And from this substance, according to certain authorities, He formed such a woman as did not please the man whom He had previously made. Then it came to pass that when God had given life to the one and to the other, Adam killed his wife, and God asked him why he had done this. He replied, "She was nothing to me and therefore I could not love her." So Our Lord came then to Adam where he slept, and took one of his ribs, and from it fashioned Eve, whence we are all descended. Wherefore some maintain that if that first woman had remained, Adam would never have yielded to the sin for which we are all in pain. (42)

In this passage we already see her sly nature (like the fox?), shaped by the lover's discourse of the late Middle Ages, in which the two Marys (Madonna and Magdalene) composed—and sadly still compose—the most decisive and stagnant dialectic in terms of the representation of women. She is obliged to be quick-witted to evade capture in turn, but to do so in a way that does not insult the wolf in sheep's clothing. Hence such brilliant rhetorical pivots as "for truly I am bound to treasure the amount of honor I have, since you are so covetous to get it" (44). Moreover, "there is no beast to be feared like the soft word that comes deceiving" (47). By hitching his portrait of passive-aggressive gender dynamics to an erotic iteration of Aesop's fables, Fournival makes a shrewd, illuminating, and rather enduring comment on the creaturely core of desire.

Returning to this sexual congress of the birds, the lady lets down her guard a little to make a direct parry: "Ah lord master, how strongly I believe that if I put my trust in you as does the ostrich in the sun, you would rear me abominably!" (52). Lessons are to be drawn from the natural world; after all, for the would-be lover with a curious eye, the birds and the bees are a primer in sexual mores, just as "the crane teaches me that I must not put any of my trust even in the most trustworthy thing in the world, and more than the crane that flies through the air" (47). What is more, this lady has no illusions about a solidarity of sisterhood, for "there are few women who have not been deceived, one through another. This is clearly signified to us by the hunters of wild birds. For I see that when they have lured one bird, they make that bird their decoy, and the other birds come to that bird and are led to capture" (55–56) (itself pointing forward to the literature of seduction in the later eighteenth century, including, and especially, Pierre Choderlos de Laclos's *Les Liasons Dangereuses*).[2] Where nature provides many models to avoid, it also produces examples worth following, as when the lady wishes that all the members of her fair sex had the good sense to be as prudent as female elephants (54).

It is a mythical creature, however, who ultimately embodies the fork-tongued suitor, who delivers such fiery words: "But to say, 'Lover, I am grieving (or dying) for you. If you do not rescue me, I am betrayed and shall die,' those words are, in my view, 'eating in the wrong way.' . . . The man who puts on such a tragic act with words belongs to the category one can rightly call The Dragons—they know how to flail around with their tongues so that they deceive poor, foolish women and with their flailing subjugate them" (54). Humans, it turns out, are unique among the animals in that body language is not enough. A woman must be forced to cross words with words, as animals do with tails or talons. At least to the slow or stubborn man, she must articulate matters, so that the tongue, one of the key organs of love, spits a type of venom of repulsion. "In my view," she finally writes, "when a person does not wish to do a thing, there are multiple refusals. Let that suffice for good understanding" (58).

# 10 THE CUCKOLD AND THE COCKATRICE
*Fourier and Hazlitt*

One of the most disturbing, and historically significant, cases of animal symbolism was deployed throughout medieval Europe to identify and dehumanize Jews. Especially from the tenth to twelfth centuries, horns were forcibly placed on the heads of people identified as Jewish, ostensibly to represent their bestial, Satanic, and unholy status in relation to the true Christian. Such blatant anti-Semitism perhaps occurred more in representations, such as drawings, or in literary descriptions than in actual life, given the logistics involved. But the motif itself reminds us that behind every case of creaturely love, there is surely also an expression of creaturely *hate*. The two passions are indeed rarely found far apart. Closer to the topic at hand, horns themselves are an ambiguous symbol in this period, sometimes signifying the virile power of the buck or stag but more often than not denoting the ignorance and/or jealousy of the cuckold.[1] The word *cuckold* originates in "the cuckoo's habit of laying its egg in another bird's nest" *(OED)*. The associated imagery of a husband "growing horns" when his wife is promiscuous refers to the mating habits of stags, who must relinquish their mate if defeated by another. Thus, in this case, the idiom "to have the horn" figuratively places a stag's antlers onto a bird's head: a bizarre medieval chimera, if ever there was one.[2]

The creaturely (read abject) status of the husband who cannot satisfy or control his wife is a universal and timeless theme—one examined with systematic zeal by libidinal socialist utopian Charles Fourier. In his rather hastily assembled and unfinished pamphlet *The Hierarchies of Cuckoldry*, Fourier (2011) provides a "zoological guidebook" to seventy-two specimens of men swept up in women's countless "secret insurrections" against the "mechanical vices" of marriage. Being an enlightened soul, the author does not simply go in for cheap jokes at the expense of the ignorant husband but rather demonstrates the manifold ways in which women—as hemmed in by patriarchy as they were by their corsets—find breathing space, fleeting freedom, or even, in some cases, a lasting compromise between lover and spouse. Fourier emphasized the carceral aspect of wedlock, more conscious than any thinker before or since of the ways in which the libidinal economy is premised on the mercantile one (which is why *The Hierarchies of Cuckoldry* has recently been published by Wakefield Press alongside a companion piece called *The Hierarchies of Bankruptcy*). Fourier was nothing if not ambitious and spent much of his life detailing the social architectonics of the "phalanstery": a pragmatic sexual utopia, eschewing all forms of ownership, especially of people; allowing equality between the sexes; and promoting maximum pleasure with minimum pain (what he called the "Harmony"). "All anarchy," he writes, "in love as in politics, leads to new order" (2011, 39).[3] Cuckoldry was thus considered by Fourier as an unfortunate and timid stage of experimentation with different affects and different partners, hobbled, however, by the moral hypocrisy and political cowardice of the age. A "half measure," as he puts it, which are always "worse than evil in that they only serve to aggravate it" (4). But despite his philosophical distaste for the deceptions involved, to the self as much as the betrothed ("cuckoldry often brings more ridicule to the lover than the husband" [xix]), he had the satirist's temperament enough to find the comical element in it as well. We can therefore read this specialized bestiary as a Swiftian footnote to his more systematic and serious writings, especially *Theory of the Four Movements and the General Destinies* (1808).

Fourier's taxonomy of horned gentleman includes "the transcendent or high-flying cuckold" (who knowingly leases his wife to another for personal gain); "the gleaner or commonplace cuckold" (who works extra hard to obtain "a slice of the pie," after others have happily eaten their fill); "the posthumous cuckold or the cuckold of two worlds" (who the world *officially* recognizes as the father of a child born ten months after he has passed away); "the cosmopolitan or hospitable cuckold" (whose house is so frequented by men from around the world that his suspicions are unable to rest upon any of them); and "the cuckold by calling or grace" (who is quite simply "the best sort of cuckold to be found in the entire fraternity" [25]). Add to this "the presumptive cuckold," who is "a man who dreads his common destiny long before the marriage, who tortures his mind in his efforts to escape it, and suffers misfortune before actually experiencing it" (10). This, in contrast to the specimen who has banished the possibility from his mind, so that "he fails to see what is taking place in his own household and would do better to keep an eye on what is growing on his forehead" (13). The misanthropic cuckold, moreover, "is a semi-madman, pitiful in his moralistic wailing, and he would have done better not to marry if he is so loath to sharing the lot of so many honest men who are his equal" (28). The variation that Fourier himself aspires to be is "the judicious, or guaranteed, protocuckold cuckold," who manages to strike with his wife "a deal for liberty, respect, protection, and reciprocal friendship" (32). This is aligned with "the preferred cuckold," for a "household is never happier than when man and woman lead this sort of life" (36). The assumption here is that monogamy is a myth that humans should not cling to but rather rewrite and transcend. (It is in this sense that Fourier is the godfather of contemporary polyamory.) Animals, historically and symbolically, have played their role here too, with swans being held aloft as the perfect role models for the ideal marriage. Science, however, is not so sentimental, demonstrating through close observation that nature too is replete with cuckolds of all descriptions (even as the notion of an animal spouse is an anthropomorphic projection).[4] Fourier's extremely specialized bestiary assumes human exceptionalism in the sense that we are the only species to have so many options at our disposal to deal with the inevitability and consequences of so-called infidelity. Yet still we look to the animal kingdom for vital metaphors of our own predicament and folly.

But what of the cockatrice—the female, far more menacing creature who excites and incites the cuckold? The cockatrice is a serpent, identified with the mythical basilisk, "said to kill by its mere glance, and to be hatched from a cock's egg." Not surprising, then, that it is also a "name of reproach for a woman: prostitute, whore" *(OED)*. Both definitions play their part in William Hazlitt's ([1823] 2007) novella *Libor Amoris: or, The New Pygmalion,* in which a gentleman lodger becomes obsessed with the young lady of the house. Despite his wary nature, and distrust of her designs, the impressionable fellow is no less caught in a tawdry, transgenerational feminine web: for "it is evident she is a practised, callous jilt, a regular lodging-house decoy, played off by her mother upon the lodgers, one after another, applying them to her different purposes, laughing at them in turns, and herself the probable dupe and victim of some favourite gallant in the end. I know all this; but what do I gain by it, unless I could find some one with her shape and air, to supply the place of the lovely apparition?" (102). A cynical or realist understanding is no armor against love:

and so she vanished in this running fight of question and answer, in spite of my vain efforts to detain her. The cockatrice, I said, mocks me: so she has always done. The thought was a dagger to me. My head reeled, my heart recoiled within me. I was stung with scorpions; my flesh crawled; I was choked with rage; her scorn scorched me like flames; her air (her heavenly air) withdrawn from me, stifled me, and left me gasping for breath and being. It was a fable. She started up in her own likeness, a serpent in place of a woman. She had fascinated, she had stung me, and had returned to her proper shape, gliding from me after inflicting the mortal wound, and instilling deadly poison into every pore; but her form lost none of its original brightness by the change of character, but was all glittering, beauteous, voluptuous grace. Seed of the serpent or of the woman, she was divine! I felt that she was a witch, and had bewitched me. Fate had enclosed me round about. *I* was transformed too, no longer human (any more than she, to whom I had knit myself) my feelings were marble; my blood was of molten lead; my thoughts on fire. I was taken out of myself, wrapt into another sphere, far from the light of day, of hope, of love. I had no natural affection left; she had slain me, but no other thing had power over me. Her arms embraced another; but her mock-embrace, the phantom of her love, still bound me, and I had not a wish to escape. So I felt then, and so perhaps shall feel till I grow old and die, nor have any desire that my years should last longer than they are linked in the chain of those amorous folds, or than her enchantments steep my soul in oblivion of all other things! I started to find myself alone—for ever alone, without a creature to love me. (93)

This is a remarkable passage, tipping into romantic kitsch, with an entire patriarchal and histrionic tradition of attraction–repulsion condensed into a single paragraph. It is, moreover, an expression of creaturely love par excellence, with its wavering between horror, fascination, human, and not (as well as a final acknowledgment that we do not necessarily mind if the being that loves us is human or not, as long as there is love and recognition). "May God bless her for not utterly disowning and destroying me!" the narrator writes. "What an exquisite little creature it is, and how she holds out to the last in her system of consistent contradictions" (73). The shift in pronoun here—from *her* to *it* and then back to *she*—is similarly instructive in its oscillation (or better, double vision) of viewing the beloved as an (un)human being.

Fourier, in contrast, was less susceptible to such masculinist fantasies of the corrupting power of Woman. (Indeed, he is credited with being the first to use the term *feminism*.) In Fourier's intricate understanding, women are the greater victims of society's hypocrisy, when it comes to the managing of human passions. Whereas the philandering of men is tolerated, women tend to "have all too few [such] distractions." For the Frenchman, "all men have penchant for polygamy," as do "civilized ladies" (Fourier 1971, 334). "Our customs and our legislation," he writes, "require a young woman to deprive herself of love until her tender father and her tender mother have found her a buyer. They oblige her to love this buyer all her life, and to love no one if there is no buyer" (334). Indeed, "there are still many parents who allow their unmarried daughters to suffer and die for want of sexual satisfaction" (336). A grim fate indeed. Instead, Fourier proposes elaborate sessions in the Courts of Love, to be held on the grounds of utopian communities known as "phalansteries," which by virtue of their collective influence will help usher in the age of Harmony. These erotic festivals are envisaged as highly orchestrated, rather theatrical, prolonged orgies, based on all manner of complicated sympathies (both physical and spiritual) between the participants. (We might think of Fourier as "the good Sade," given their shared mania for choreographing desirable and desiring bodies.) "Only by satisfying the need for physical love, will it become possible to guarantee the development of the noble element in love" (339), he writes. Fourier's proto-Reichian philosophy is thus based on the need for physical, bodily satisfaction—what he calls the "social minimum"—guaranteed to all in his erotic democracy.

For inspiration, he turned from his home city of Lyon to the French capital, for here "the courtesans" and "social lions" of Paris understand that "conjugal intolerance is bad form at the court and in society." Just as eating furtively alone is, for Fourier, to behave like an animal, making love in private, with one's legal partner, is—by inference—to operate on a subhuman level. This connoisseur of civilized Eros was not at all interested in returning to a more immediate, animalistic form of desire. While the passions are indeed originally dictated by nature, in his view, physical pleasure is a social art: one that will become infinitely more noble and enriching once we banish the scandal of interpersonal possession via wedlock (barely one step above human slavery). Here we might recall Nietzsche's (1989) important point from *On the Genealogy of Morals*: "To breed an animal *with the right to make promises*—is not this the paradoxical task that nature has set itself in the case of man? is it not the real problem regarding man?" (57). Certainly one of the most weighty promises any of us will make to our fellow man (or woman) is to promise to remain faithful to him (or her), spoken during the wedding ceremony in a supreme instance of the consequential speech act. In Fourier's view, no animal would be foolish enough to put itself in such a position, because even the beast in the field instinctively knows that tastes and situations change. Moreover, no being should somehow "belong" to another. Nor should any civilized being expect another to make a promise—let alone keep it. Indeed, to recognize the protean nature of desire (that is to say, the protean desires of nature) would be the more *moral* path to take, perhaps for Nietzsche, as much as for Fourier.

In the figure of the cuckold, especially, Fourier was insightful enough to recognize the creaturely element within the human affairs of his epoch. Unfortunately, he was also such a typical product of this high-humanist century that he looked forward to transcending any and all animalistic tendencies, thereby altogether missing the very many possible ways in which a sophisticated acknowledgment of the creaturely aspect of erotic encounters might inspire or enhance refined and rewarding love making in the age of Harmony. Instead, Fourier believed that those proverbial antlers growing on the forehead of duped husbands could simply be shed en masse and left behind in the troubled gardens of domesticity, soon to be bleached by the summery dawn of a new and enlightened sensual species.

# 11 THE ANIMAL BRIDE AND HORNY TOADS

Figuring the beloved as an animal is a universal motif, with a history as long as humanity's own. In traditional myths, legends, and folktales, cross-species romance is taken for granted, as in the "animal bride" story found throughout the world's oldest narratives. As intellectual historian Boria Sax (1998) notes in his excellent book on this theme, all such tales of creaturely matrimony follow a similar structure or shape: "An animal takes on the form of a woman. A man wins her love and, for a while, they live harmoniously as husband and wife. They have children. One day, the husband makes an error or violates a prohibition. The wife reverts to her bestial form and leaves, taking the children with her" (5). In such accounts, Sax argues, the husband represents humanity, the bride symbolizes the natural world, and their marriage embodies the fraught and fragile relationship between these two realms.[1] The animal bride story tells of the ongoing historical project of domestication: a process that is never guaranteed to go smoothly, whether we are talking about animals, human partners, or, indeed, ourselves. (Being "house trained" is, after all, as challenging for some people as it is for some puppies—in the bedroom as much as the bathroom.)

If we place, say, Master Richard's *Bestiary,* or, indeed, Fourier's, within such a lineage, we can see how creaturely love has been depicted in and by different epochs to comment on perceived ontological differences, at the same time gaining a sense of the way cultures and individuals attempt to navigate these differences. One remarkable aspect of the animal bride story is that it seems to presume that it is easier to change genus than gender. "Sex, in much of folklore," writes Sax, "can be a difference even more intractable than that of species" (22). Gender has therefore been considered in pre- and early modern times to be *the* great existential divide, far more significant than the one that has been given more emphasis in our own time: that between the human and the rest of the biological kingdom. It is as if Lacan's famous dictum—"there is no sexual relationship"— found its most resonant allegorical depiction in folkloric tales of uncanny alliances, missed encounters, shed skins, and melancholic misunderstandings[2] (a theme updated in the 1980s in Richard Donner's kitsch, yet suggestive, film *Ladyhawke*, in which two lovers cannot meet as humans, because they are under an evil spell that renders one a bird of prey at dawn and the other a black wolf at dusk).[3] The animal is enlisted in such instances to amplify the gender gap, "a barrier between human beings that renders communication both more difficult and more intriguing" (22).

Quoting one of Lévi-Strauss's original indigenous sources, Sax identifies the animal bride as a totem ancestor: "We know what the animals do, what are the needs of the beaver, the bear, the salmon, and other creatures, because long ago men married them and acquired this knowledge from their animal wives" (31).[4] The difference between a non-Western myth of creaturely love and one in the mode penned by Master Richard can be measured by the degree to which the latter channels a sense of loss: loss for a time in which humans and animals inhabit the same world. In the West, one would have to go back before the pre-Socratics to find such a tale spoken of without nostalgia for a vanished continuity, in which "animals and human beings are conceived simply as different tribes joined through matrimony" (29). Despite this chronology away from shared libidinal existence, however, modern narratives still bear the traces of our totemic genealogy. Indeed, totemism, for Sax (and, indeed, for our own purposes), "is not a stage of history but a way of thinking." Even today's urban folk, Sax argues, retain an animistic understanding of the world. And these are "sanctioned by myths and fairy tales, in which all beings interact on a single plane" (33).

As Sax goes on to note:

> modern culture is based on sharp divisions between the realms of people, animals, plants, and objects. While people recognized these distinctions intellectually, the distinctions have never really been internalized. They do not describe our perceptions and responses. We can manipulate people as objects. We can talk to plants. The proliferation of sentimental entertainments in modern times is partly due to the tension between humanistic philosophies and our still largely animistic perception of the world. (151–52)

While humans may construct their own "symbolic" reality, they do so with the assistance of animals and other life-forms.[5] And yet we also constantly disavow this fact: a disavowal that shapes one of the strongest and most consistent habits of mind of modernity and its aftermath. "In humanism," Sax writes, "man becomes his own totem, his own companion, ancestor, and god. He can be anything but himself." However, "humanism cannot give man an identity, since it does not know any significant point of orientation apart from human beings" (181). Stories of interspecies marriage can as a consequence be read as a general collective protest about the increasing ideological distance cast between ourselves and our fellow creatures (whereby the notion of "fellowship" is recognized less and less as history "progresses").

And yet, reminders of this wider kinship persist in our own rituals and vocabulary. For Sax, "the similarity between romantic love and marriage on the one hand and pet-keeping on the other is striking. Both are bonds of potentially enormous intensity, involving mutual sharing and affection. We even call the endearments used by lovers 'pet names,' since they are often terms for animals. Sexual play short of intercourse is often referred to as 'petting'" (25). Indeed, when we dress up for a romantic date, we might reach for an outfit made of leather, fur, or—depending on the time, place, and inclination—even feathers. It is as if we feel incomplete in our own skin and need to supplement our all-too human desires with creaturely supplements or prostheses: an elaborate zootechnical apparatus designed to augment the creature without qualities. Part of this particular tool kit is the symbolic association of romantic pursuit with the hunt: a trope stretching from antiquity to contemporary subcultures who talk of women as "targets" or "game." For Sax, again, "we easily forget that the bow and arrow held by Eros or Cupid in allegories of love is a weapon for hunting and war. For people of the ancient world, erotic love inspired far less gentleness than conflict" (99). (Cupid himself, in Roman depictions, was often given the wings of a bird, before Renaissance paintings made his flight far less pagan, afforded by angel feathers.) The metamorphoses of Zeus, ravishing his sexual prey in the guise of a swan or a bull, comprise a violent adjunct to the more consensual domestic scene of animal bride stories. Especially notable, then, is the dearth of examples in which the many goddesses living in the Pantheon were tempted into following his example, morphing into an animal to mate with a mortal man. This reticence on a goddess's part may be because a woman, immortal or not, is—according to the gendered subtexts of Occidental culture—already too close to the creature on the symbolic spectrum, and thus such a transformation would be redundant or tautological.

The shifting border line between human and animal has—like the Berlin Wall—been policed with greater vigilance at different times and at different checkpoints. Unlike the Berlin Wall, however, it has yet to be dismantled, even as the cultural confidence in humanist mantras erodes at an increasingly rapid rate, thanks to the advances in scientific discovery and evolving trends in posthumanistic thought. Sax tells us that "during late medieval times, as the boundary between the human and animal realms came to seem less secure, bestiality was condemned with increasing severity" (107). Women were also tried and executed as witches, sometimes for the sole reason of talking to their cats. Creaturely love was therefore particularly taboo at this stage of history. However, an interest in potential affections between species rebounds with great energy in the early modern period—as repressed ideas are wont to do (102). In his "Apology for Raymond Sebond," for instance—"possibly the most extensive collection of animal anecdotes in early modern times" (Sax 1998, 102)—Montaigne discusses several examples of the amorous designs of beasts on people. "Witness the elephant," he writes, "who was rival to Aristophanes the grammarian in the love of a young flower girl in the city of Alexandria, and who yielded no ground to him in the attentions of a very passionate suitor . . . and every day are seen monkeys furiously in love with women" (in Sax 1998, 102–3). Sax notes that while Montaigne considers such passions "unnatural," he "never questions the depth or authenticity of the love" (103). Animal bride stories provide an archetypal provenance for these more "liberal" views of proto-Darwinian romance, paving the way for a future in which not only are animals considered more human but humans are (re)considered as merely one—albeit eccentric—type of animal. "Stories of the animal bride or groom are our purest fairy tales," writes Sax. "They tell of a perfect love, able to triumph over weakness, foolishness, and even death. They also acknowledge that human society is not necessarily where such love is to be found" (161).[6] One useful addendum, then, to Sax's fascinating study of the animal bride and her discursive daughters is the following syllogism: "All humans are animals. All brides are humans. Therefore, all brides are animals." In other words, the bride is *always* an animal bride. The groom is *always* an animal groom. And this holds true, whether these brides or grooms were, up until the wedding ceremony, a horse or a graphic designer.

As fairy tales reveal to us, the groom may also be first found in the form of an amphibian. The classic Brothers Grimm tale of "The Frog King"—in which a princess must first contend with a horny toadlike creature before he is shown to be a handsome prince under a wicked spell—is yet another tacit acknowledgment of our own creaturely loves (and aversions). Reading this story, it is difficult to see the covetous frog—who would have the beautiful young woman share her bed with him in return for rescuing her golden ball from the pond—as anything other than an allegory of the kind of old and warty figure to whom many a maiden was betrothed, against her will. The sudden and unexpected transformation, then, is an expression of wish fulfilment for both character and reader, who implicitly understand that beauty should not be shackled to ugliness. (In the Grimm version, the change occurs after the princess throws the frog against the bedroom wall in disgust and not—as popular culture now has it—through a kiss.) For folklorist and medievalist Beryl Rowland (1973, viii), the frog is thus a "symbol of sexual initiation," given its phallic tongue, slimy texture, and rather belligerent, grotesque manner. Creaturely love, let us remind ourselves, is not all swanlike maidens and panther-like men. It can just as often be embodied in a wheezing bullfrog, with the sticky finger pads and curling, gibblety lips reminiscent of one's creepy uncle. (Consider how the phrase "who was that *creature* you were with last night?!" can, through different emphasis, be an expression of envious wonder or appalled contempt.)

In any case, the genre of the medieval bestiary provides a rich and heavily coded tapestry of animal types, blissfully unconfined by the cages of Linnaean taxonomy. Rather, they were arranged by symbolic import; itself never fixed, so that a single animal can represent polar opposites of the moral spectrum, depending on the text (for instance, religious or vulgar) and context (place, time, and purpose). As Rowland notes, the word *symbol* itself comes from the Greek phrase "to throw together," and there is a kind of ongoing Doctor Moreauesque experiment going on in texts of the Middle Ages, splicing animals together for allegorical or simply comical effect. More often than not, however, the animal in premodern writing and iconography was the opportunity for "a sermon in shorthand" (xvi)—animals being close enough to humans to recognize their key characteristics but far away enough to draw lessons from this distance and difference, inscribed by God.

Consider, for instance, the English cleric Edward Topsell, whose volume *The Histoire of Foure-Footed Beasts and Serpents* (1607) became a relatively late contribution to the medieval bestiary, while also serving as a reflection upon the history of such. Topsell looks back to the ancient Roman writer Apuleius, whose most famous work described a man whose ill-informed dabbling in magic results in being transformed into a donkey. According to the cleric,

> Apuleius in his eleven bookes of his golden Asse taketh that beast for an Emblem, to note the manners of mankind; how some by youthful pleasures become beasts. . . . Some are in their lives Wolves; some Foxes, some Swine, some Asses. . . . This world is unto them an enchanted cup of Circes, wherein they drinke up a potion of oblivion, error and ignorance; afterwards brutizing in their whole life, till they taste the Roses of true science and grace enlightening their minds. (in Rowland 1973, 23)

Yet again, humans are closer to animals, until such time as they see the light of the Lord (and, in this early Enlightenment text, the "Roses of true science")—which is why they are so instructive, in a time when the Christian "flock" was considered more than simply a metaphor (given that the lamb of Christ could also arrive in the form of an actual lamb . . . that is, when not doing double-duty as shepherd).

The affective indiscipline of the animal is what was most disconcerting for the moralists of the Middle Ages, and of the Elizabethan age that followed. Topsell believed, for instance, that "there is no beast that is more prone and given to lust than is a goate" (in Rowland 1973, 80). Hence the ancient figure of the satyr—half-man and half-goat—who in pagan times was a figure of Dionysian joys and pursuits but, in the Christian era, soon served as "a terrible warning of what a man would become if he surrendered himself to carnal desire" (81). Certainly others may find cause to distrust foxes or dogs to the same degree as a goat. As Rowland points out,

> medieval priests, taxed with the burden of regulating the sex life of their flocks, found the dog's sexual habits a useful kind of yardstick whereby to elicit information of a most intimate kind. At confession the priest would bluntly ask the penitent before him whether he had copulated with his wife like a dog. The penalty for such an offense, according to Burchard, bishop of Worms early in the eleventh century, was ten days on bread and water. . . . Other details concerning the canine mode of copulation were deemed to be appropriately retributive: a typical afterlife punishment for illicit lovers

was for them to be joined *quomodo canis* and to whirl around hell for all eternity. (60)

As wild dogs, wolves also steal into the language as creaturely imposters of the libidinal economy within domestication, as the "Little Red Riding Hood" story attests. In France, for instance, it is still said of a virgin girl that she "n'a jamais vu le loup."[7] Indeed, for Rowland, animals are such potent symbols because they are "the indirect representation of sexual wishes. The transformation of the animal into a human represents the overcoming of resistance to sexuality: the breaking of the spell is a release from guilt" (86). While we may bristle at the facile Freudian reading of such stories, it nevertheless contains an intriguingly counterintuitive logic. *To refuse sex is to remain an animal.* One must thus *learn* to be fully human by "making love" in a pious manner, somehow different to the godless rutting of the beasts. (A lesson not fully absorbed by Aristotle, according to legend, for the great philosopher of natural history and animal types was said to be so besotted with the Queen of Greece that he allowed her to straddle him like a horse.)[8]

Once again, the animal proves to have at least two sides, and for every heartening reconciliation between princess and frog, there is a disturbing gendered conflict that calls for allegorical solutions:

> From the sixteenth to the nineteenth century, a nagging woman might be punished by having the scold's bridle, an iron noose, slipped over her head. The bit held down her tongue, and the noose often had a chain and a ring attached so that the woman could be led about like a horse. One such contraption, preserved in Walton Church and said to be dated 1633, bore the inscription: "Chester presents Walton with a bridle / To curb women's tongues that talk too idle." The symbolism persists to today in the marriage ceremony, in which the ring is the halter used by the groom to harness his bride. (105)[9]

One imagines that many a heartless husband dismissed the distress of his wife as mere "crocodile tears."[10]

# 12 UNSETTLED BEING

*Ovid's Metamorphoses*

The fluidity of medieval species-being—the cosmology whereby a creature can transform into something radically different or combine into fantastic hybrids in the popular imaginary (and thus become an exhibit in proto-zoological treatises)—can be traced back in the Western tradition to the poet laureate of protean forms, Ovid. In his magnificent compendium of mythical tales, *Metamorphoses,* no character, human or otherwise, can ever take for granted its current shape or nature. A woman might suddenly turn into a tree, a bear, a bird, a bat, a mare, a cow, or even some marsh reeds or a mountain spring. A man might find himself suddenly transfigured into a bull, a stag, a snake, or a frog, while star-crossed couples can, perhaps appropriately, mutually morph into a stellar constellation. In Ovid's account, humans evolved from stones in one description and mushrooms in another. Meanwhile, one of the gods' favorite sports is to disguise themselves as specific animals—rams, bulls, horses, swans, serpents—to have their way with hapless but alluring mortals.[1] Ovid's world is aggressively and relentlessly in flux: a radically unstable ontology based on a promiscuous and prescientific narrative of genesis and genus.[2] As such, it manages to eschew what Leo Bersani calls (with some disdain) "settled being" (Bersani and Dutoit 2008, 9).

What triggers such changes? Often a change happens as punishment, due to a sexual transgression or else, as in the case of Olympians, to enjoy one. On other occasions, the shift is to avoid being trespassed upon. Metamorphoses can also occur as a consequence of an intense affective surge, such as grief, or jealousy, or shame. Very often it is desire itself that leads directly to a sudden transformation, as if the new incarnation was somehow dormant within the original creature, just waiting for the right moment of impassioned heat to spark the change. But whatever the logic or trigger for one character being transposed into another, this poetic encyclopedia of ancient tales provides a wealth of examples of creaturely love, many of which set the stage and the tone for two thousand years of discourse concerning Eros and its others—all the way up to the modernist variations that we have touched upon in previous chapters. Some vignettes, however, complicate the erotic dynamic between human and not-human in sophisticated ways from the beginning. That is to say, Ovid seems to anticipate some of the ways in which sex, gender, and species *trouble* identity rather than acting as the flagship principles on which it tries to construct itself (foundational concepts such as essence, soul, conatus, ego, ipseity, integrity, and related names we give to the presumption of the self's continuity through time, at least until death).

Love, in Ovid's hands, is not a gentle and many-splendored thing but a catalytic trauma, described as "Cupid's spiteful resentment" (Ovid 2004, 28). Cupid himself has two types of arrow: "one is for rousing passion, the other is meant to repel it"—the former gold, the latter lead (28–29). Evidently it pleases the mischievous cherub to mess with people's hearts and minds. In the Greco-Roman world, "unrequited love" is a tautology, and the gods go to great lengths to make sure that it is born of asymmetry and incompatibility. (It is in this sense that Ovid's tales can be read retrospectively as Lacanian fables: a tragicomedy of failed pursuits, illusory possessions, and missed encounters.)[3]

Consider the case of Jupiter, "father and ruler of all the gods," who disguises himself as a bull to seduce the Tyrian princess Európa:

> There wasn't a threat in his brow or a fearsome glare in his
>     eyes;
> his face was a picture of perfect peace. The Princess Európa
> gazed in wonder upon this gentle and beautiful creature.
> At first, despite his unthreatening looks, she was
>     frightened to touch him;
> but soon she approached with a garland of flowers for
>     his gleaming head.
> Her lover was blissful and licked her hands as a
>     prelude to other
> and sweeter pleasures, pleasures he barely, barely
>     could wait for.
> Now he would gambol beside her, prancing around on
>     the green grass;

now he would rest his snow-white flank in the golden
   sand.
As little by little her fears were allayed, he would
      offer his front
to be stroked by her maidenly hand or his horns to be
   decked with fresh garlands.
The princess even ventured to sit with her legs astride
on the back of the bull, unaware whose sides she was
      resting her thighs on;
when Jupiter, gradually edging away from the land and
      away
from the dry shore, placed his imposter's hooves in the
   shallowest waves,
then advanced further, and soon he was bearing
      the spoils of his victory
out in mid-ocean. His frightened prize looked back at
   the shore
she was leaving behind, with her right hand clutching
   one horn and her left
on his back for support, while her fluttering dress
swelled out in the breeze. (89–90)

Clearly there is a strong allegorical and erotic power to this scene, in which
a young woman is misled by appearances and left all "at sea" by a duplici-
tous beast. It speaks of the long and ongoing history of men pretending
they are something they are not to get that thing they desire (a duplicity
that can itself provide the *frisson* for women who daydream about being
misled in just such a fashion).[4] Which is to say that in Ovid's world, it is
the creatural that has a sexual advantage over the merely mortal and is
more likely to sneak under the defenses of a would-be chaste maiden. And
love is not a blessing of the gods but rather a sign that one of the immortal
want you as his plaything, or is simply against you.[5]

   While it is true that male figures are usually the active, even predatory
partners, in Ovid's world, the poet is sure to provide several examples
of desirous females, who either love beyond measure, like Echo, or who
lust with a keen and ingenious determination, as in the case of Pasiphaë.
This latter case also involves a bull, so alluring in its simple libidinal presence that it inflames the half-divine, half-nymphic daughter of the Sun.
The bull has eyes only for its own kind, however, so Pasiphaë employs a

scandalous subterfuge: commissioning a wooden cow, within which she crouches in her creatural lust, to successfully trick the beast into mounting her (300–301, 376)—an unnatural coupling that leads to the birth of the Minotaur.

Less overtly bestial is the story of Salmacis—"the only naiad not to belong to the train of Diana." (And it is highly significant that women who take the erotic initiative are almost always more-than-mortal.) Nevertheless, in a refreshing reversal of the usual voyeuristic scenario, Salmacis spies a handsome youth, Hermaphroditus, bathing in a sparkling pool and tries her best to woo him with words and the natural charms of her carriage and costume. When this only makes the naive lad blush, she becomes impatient with "her quarry" and ravishes him:

> For all his valiant attempts to slip from her grasp, she
>> finally
> held him tight in her coils, like a huge snake carried aloft
> in an eagle's talons, forming knots round the head and the
>> feet
> of the royal bird and entangling the flapping wings in its
>> tail;
> or like the ivy which weaves its way round the length of a
>> tree-trunk,
> or else an octopus shooting all its tentacles out
> to pounce on its prey and maintain its grip in the depths of
>> the sea. (148–49)

Still, he resists, obliging Salmacis to send a prayer up to Olympia:

> "... Gods, I pray you,
>> decree
> that the day never comes when the two of us here shall be
>> riven asunder!"
> Her prayer found gods to fulfil it. The bodies of boy and
>> girl
> were merged and melded in one. The two of them showed
>> but a single
> face. (149)

Hence the origin of our term *hermaphrodite*, "described as male or as female. They seemed to be neither and both." This new human fusion is an exceptional transgendered figure, who perhaps could only find a kindred spirit in Teiresias, one of the very few individuals who had "experienced love from both angles" (108) and who famously pronounced the female experience of sexual pleasure to be many times more intense than the male. We might recall here the subtextual moral of the animal bride story: that species is an easier bridge to cross than gender. Though swapping genders is not impossible, Ovid's poem seems to similarly suggest that such a process is somehow more significant than changing species, or even phylum, or domain. Given the very many metamorphoses in the fifteen books, it appears easier—and far more likely—for men to spring from fungi, or women to spasm into bats, than for a man to become a woman, or vice versa.

One such exceptional tale involves the figure of Iphis, who is born a girl but raised as a boy (to evade those who would kill a daughter out of ideological spite). Iphis becomes betrothed to a young woman and falls deeply in love with her. The anxiety surrounding the impending ceremony and wedding night creates a crisis in this ancient cross-dresser, who appeals to the natural world for a solution to the "monstrous" nature of her predicament. "Cows never burn with desire for cows, nor mares for mares," she thinks gloomily to herself.

> Ewes are attracted to rams and every stag has his hind;
> the same with the mating of birds. Throughout the
>    animal kingdom
> the female is never smitten with passionate love for a
> female.
> I wish I had never been born a woman, I wish I were
>    dead!
> But Crete is the land of every perversion. Pasíphaë
>    lusted
> after a bull—but her love was a male. My passion is
> wilder
> than that, if the truth be told . . .
> . . .
>
> O Juno, goddess of marriage, O Hymen! Why are you
>    gracing
> a wedding between two brides (377)

In this case, Iphis's prayers are answered, and the divine sex change operation is granted in time, ensuring that this new man is no longer obliged to transgress the natural law of gendered intercourse. (Itself an ideological fantasy, as several recent ethological studies have shown. Nature, it is increasingly revealed, is not the ur-text of our own historical bias toward heterosexual coupling but a queer heterotopia, "pink in tooth and claw," perverse only when viewed from a reductionist and moral view of sexual behavior.)[6]

More complex and controversial still is Ovid's treatment of incest, a recurrent theme in Greek and Roman mythology. For influential cultural thinkers like Lévi-Strauss and Freud, the incest taboo is the original and founding sign of the shift from nature to culture (and thus the origin of the human). It is the inchoate invention of law, which distinguishes the humanoid animal from the human proper. In Ovid, such stories seem to be reflecting on this irreversible breach between *nomos* and *phusis,* upon which the Greeks were among the first to reflect (at least in writing). The key story in this case is that of Byblis, Apollo's grandchild, who falls desperately in love with her twin brother and, as a consequence, wavers between confusion and confession. Long before the iPad, Byblis has recourse to her "tablet" for communicating to her forbidden lover-brother:

> With trembling fingers she scratched the words she had
>     formed in her mind,
> her right hand guiding the pen and her left controlling the
>     tablet.
> She'd start and she'd stop; she'd write on the wax, then
>     curse what she'd written;
> inscribing and then deleting, emending, rejecting,
> approving; (365)[7]

But her agonized love letter is only met with horror, and she becomes so distraught that she dissolves into ashamed tears—literally—and flows away into a stream:

> Had Byblis befriended Myrrha, mother of Adonis, she would have at least had a kindred spirit for immoral support. For Myrrha felt a great erotic attraction to her father, Cinyras, the king of Cyprus. (It appears she cannot blame Cupid, however, for this passion, since he himself denies that his arrows were her downfall.) [397]

"All other creatures can mate as they choose for themselves," she laments to herself.

. . . It isn't considered a
    scandal for bulls
to mount the heifers they've sired or for stallions to
    serve their own fillies;
goats may cover the young that they've spawned, and
    even a bird
can conceive her chicks by a mate who happens to be
    her father.
How lucky they are to do as they please! How
    spitefully human
morality governs our lives! What nature freely allows
    us,
the jealous law will refuse. (398)

Myrrha's "unnatural desires" are thus rationalized as the most natural of all: the impulse of the innocent animals in the fields. Civilization is thus condemned as an estrangement from "a natural love . . . intensified by the double attachment." The conflicting role of nature is exposed in this tortured—but extremely common—logic, whereby the animals are both Innocents and Monsters, depending on the discourse being deployed and the ideological reasons for doing so. In any case, after tricking her father, under cover of night, into making love with her, Myrrha is punished for her transgression by being turned into a tree, so that her profane body does not pollute the earth below.

# 13 FICKLE METAPHYSICS

One important thing to note about Ovid's specific depiction of metamorphosis is the way in which the altered subject both *is*, and *is* no longer, the self-same as before. Myrrha is thus still affected by shame and grief, even after becoming a tree, with the resin of her tears to prove it. Consider also Acteaon, who is transformed in the midst of hunting into a stag by a furious Diana and thus is torn to shreds by his own dogs, who do not recognize "him." The fact that the young man can witness his own ironic death is evidence that Acteon is still, at some level, Acteon. This is key when we reach the final book in Ovid's epic poem, where Pythagoras makes a decisive cameo appearance—a kind of deus ex machina—to explain all the Orphic and metamorphic mysteries that came before and give them an ethical import.

According to the ventriloquized philosopher: "All is in flux / Any shape that is formed is constantly / shifting." We can find comfort and orientation, however, in the fact that "our souls, however, are free from death. They simply / depart / from their former homes and continue their lives in new / habitations" (Ovid 2004, 601).[1] In other words,

Nothing at all in the world can perish. . . .
things merely vary and change their appearance. What
    we call birth
is merely becoming a different entity; what we call
    death
is ceasing to be the same. Though the parts may
    possibly shift
their position from here to there, the wholeness in
    nature is constant. (606)

The more things change, the more they stay the same—at least from a true philosophical perspective. And it is from this continuity-within-difference where Ovid's stories get their great pathos and energy. (And this is why Pythagoras beseeches us to be vegetarian—so we do not unwittingly devour one of our ancestors or even a recently departed friend or family member.)[2] If Inachus's daughter had simply been turned into a "snow-white heifer," then there would be no more tale to tell. But the fact that she still recognizes her father after the transformation, and he recognizes her, makes the scene where she tearfully licks his fingers and he feeds her grass more poignant. The same applies when Apollo can still feel Daphne's heart-beat fluttering beneath the hard bark her formerly silky skin has become.[3]

Thus Ovid's universe—in which "no one's favour is lasting" (67)—is animated by constant change: a fickle metaphysics. And yet beneath all this flux lies not only the indestructability of the soul but the eternal nature of certain passions or sorrows (as with the lonely voice of Echo or the amber tears of forever-grieving woman-trees).[4] No wonder psychoanalysis found tales like this to be such a rich resource for understanding modern neuroses, with its vivid and detailed panorama of repetition and compulsion, acting out and working through, misrecognitions and defense mechanisms. But just as Freud and his followers projected their own explanatory apparatus back onto Narcissus and others, we could also say that Ovid projects such themes *forward* to our own time, in which the plight of the ravished and abandoned, or the besotted and rejected, still has many lessons to teach us mortals.[5]

One such lesson is as difficult to assimilate as it is easy to identify, coming as it does on every page of the text, namely, the protean nature of the beloved. The creature you love is liable to be a different creature on your next encounter (or even a bit later in *this* encounter). A shy dove may swiftly morph into a ravenous bird of prey, or an old goat may transform, after a few feeble bleats, into a sleeping puppy. A mischievous nymph may suddenly become a cold slab of stone. And yet, as we have established, there is something of the former persisting within the new, or else the change would be definitive and intractable. Metamorphosis may be vexing, but it prompts a concerted search for the previous form or for the common element linking two very different forms. Indeed, the curiosity or will to knowledge that both inspires and frustrates such a search goes under the name of love—a love that scans from creature to creature.

Perhaps Ovid's greatest aesthetic achievement—which has implications far beyond "mere" aesthetics—is to push his stories to the point where metaphor is *literally* transfigured. Thus, someone who acts in a manner, say, "like a wounded bull" (349) suddenly truly turns into a wounded bull! The analogical miraculously becomes the actual. Reality and its representation collapse together and fuse. And while this may be the very conceit that classifies Ovid as a writer of myth rather than natural history, it captures a truth at the heart of creaturely love. Human passions are not simply *like* animalistic ones but are indeed an expression of them. Alterity is not only an excluded other but a latent aspect of identity, poised to become manifest at any moment (in the other as much as the self). What's more, Ovid's philosophy or cosmology shares some insights with modern biology, as informed by astrophysics. "We are star stuff," says the pop-scientific mantra, just as Ovid maintains that humans came from clay and retain the minerals of this heritage. In whatever form we find "ourselves" today, we will no doubt emerge in another next time around. The recycling of elements, and the indestructability of matter, is an established scientific principle. What Ovid does is simply speed up the action, so that it happens in a poetic temporality rather than a mundane one. And although this particular mixing of type with type is fanciful and impossible, it affords great insight on a different level, already mentioned, where analogy is understood as metaphysics wearing a mask. To remove this mask is to look squarely into the face of a radically democratic, even orgiastic, existence, marked by a blending of forms, itself the irony of a life that seeks ever to define them, one from the other. (Once again, "we are all anagrams of each other.")[6] Ovid's world depicts an "unfinished universality," according to Kaja Silverman (2009, 1–2), in which "every phenomenal form rhymes with many others" and "everything derives from the same flesh."[7]

If a person whimpers "like a dog," of course that doesn't mean he is actually a dog. But whimpering itself creates a bridge, momentarily linking human and dog. It is transductive. This is what allows empathy to happen, not only across species but across two individuals of any sufficiently sentient type (what Derrida calls "capital beings"). Thus we may also say, "You are just like Karen." That doesn't mean you *are* Karen, but the resemblance is notable and establishes a potential connection between you and her. The key existential locus or fracture is thus not between species but between individuated entities. All analogies create virtual pathways of prospective recognition and thus possible communication (or silent respect). Love may metamorphose quickly into hate. Life may metamorphose suddenly into death. But in the meantime, it is the flux that we are in the midst of, and must negotiate, by multiplying analogies as makeshift valences between people and experiences, rather than sealing them off, with a constant appeal to incommensurable differences. For although these latter certainly exist, they should not be taken as an excuse to avoid an encounter that would itself create a third term (think of how music or wordless play or physical love transcends language). This was Simondon's great insight: that the asymptotic interaction between individuals itself always creates another instance of individuation—that of the "event" of this very interaction.[8]

Several names have been bestowed on this generating matrix of (potential) resemblances by the philosophical tradition, as well as the singular, individuating expressions or instances that (temporarily) emerge from it, before plunging back into formlessness. Heidegger simply called it Being, in contrast to "beings"—an ontological gap inaugurated by Plato's metaphysical system of ideal transcendent Forms, casting shadows of appearance here on earth. The background to which the drama of *Dasein* unfolds was also informed by Aristotle's distinction between Life and the "living," whereby the latter represent a heterogeneous excrescence of the homogenous constituent of life. The Scholastics called it "prime matter": the substance that awaits its animation into univocal (or equivocal) forms. [9] Spinoza simply called it God, or nature, or essence—a monist plane or plenum from which the *conatus* of the individual gets its negentropic energy. (Leibniz would in effect grant *only* the individuals: monads floating atomistically, yet harmonically, in a vacuum, without positing a virtual reservoir from which they crumble and auto-resurrect.) Deleuze called it the "Fold," whereby an eternal becoming is evidenced through an ontological origami. The molar-being is thus a fleeting snapshot of the molecular-vector (a notion influenced in part by Gabriel Tarde, and process philosophers like Whitehead, who used a somewhat different vocabulary). The recent speculative realists, inspired by Manuel De Landa, describe it as a "flat ontology," not wishing to sweep away material differences but to emphasize the nonhierarchical nature of What Is, so that objects (including objects that flatter themselves that they are subjects) extend off over the horizon rather than up into the theologically tinted sky. One recent name is simply the "Mesh."[10] Indeed, the history of Western metaphysics—including its ongoing attempt to overcome its own errors—can be reduced to the stakes within this wager that all the "somethings" we contend with every day (friends, enemies, pets, viruses, toasters, whatever) emerge as material avatars from, and of, a more primal or profound Not-Nothing. As such, taxonomy is inherently political or moralistic, given that it attempts to fix, explain, or even justify differences that have a deeper affinity when viewed from the correct existential angle. (Hence the renewed interest in the symbolic power of the "generic" or the "whatever" in some conceptual circles.)[11]

What Ovid does is remind us that *all* recognizable figures in this world, of this earth, can be placed within the one, same demographic category. We are all "carbon heat traps": at least those characters with enough animation, presence, or charisma to appear in Ovid's cast list.[12] Once again, X is not Y. But X and Y may both share something in common with Z (even beyond an essential alphabetic-ness). Moths are flying leaves. Butterflies are flying flowers. Morton Bay fig trees are stationary elephants (or elephants are fig trees in motion). Lorikeets are rainbows trapped in bird-shaped prisms. Banksia brushes sprout affixed hedgehogs. All of nature enfolds, echoes, mimics, and refrains. And what we bracket off as "culture"—including Ovid's poems—is shown to be something we did not suspect: not a *break* from nature but a further folding of it. A complication. An enveloped "exception." That is to say, a generalized and accelerated evolution toward making the always already machinic nature of Nature explicit and formalized (what has been referred to as "tool-being").[13] It is the shiny quality of these new tools that blinds us to the natural origin and mandate of artifice or of technics in the widest sense (whereby a rotating seed pod inspires a helicopter blade, for instance). And thus our first operation—our first properly human machine—was designed to draw arbitrary lines in the sand. Lines between us and them.

In the final scenes of David Malouf's (1981) beautiful novella *An Imaginary Life,* the aging and exiled Ovid falls into the wet sand, far from his beloved Rome, and feels himself being tugged inexorably toward the ultimate metamorphosis of death. "We are continuous with earth in all the particles of our physical being," he thinks to himself, embracing the earth, almost as a lover, "as in our breathing we are continuous with sky. Between our bodies and the world there is unity and commerce" (147). Indeed,

> what else should our lives be but a continual series of beginnings, of painful settings out into the unknown, pushing off from the edges of consciousness into the mystery of what we have not yet become, except in dreams that blow in from out there bearing the fragrance of islands we have not yet sighted in our waking hours, as in voyaging sometimes the first blossoming branches of our next landfall come bumping against the keel, even in the dark, whole days before the real land rises to meet us. (135–36)

# 14 NYMPHOMANIA AND FAUNICATION

In one of his now classic methodological moves, Giorgio Agamben alerts us to the existence of an obscure and esoteric historical text that apparently sheds an entirely new light on a rather shadowy universal and timeless problem. One such text deployed for this purpose is the early sixteenth-century treatise by Paracelsus *De nymphis, sylphis, pygmeis et salamndris et caeteris spiritibus* (A Book on Nymphs, Sylphs, Pygmies and Salamanders, and on the Other Spirits). For Agamben (2011d), those nymphs that play such a significant role in Ovid's metamorphic tales also hold a privileged place in the Western tradition, because "the history of the ambiguous relation between men and nymphs is the history of the difficult relation between man and his images" (75). The philosopher's logic for such a claim is, as always, extremely nuanced, elusive, and complex. Suffice to say that the nymph is a figure that crystallizes the dialectic (or perhaps ongoing conflict) between the intellect and the imagination in human endeavors, especially in the grand epistemic break where the medieval gave way to the modern. (Agamben is not incredulous to grand narratives.) The nymph is thus a gendered creature who both represents and helps co-create aesthetic production. She is a mythical avatar who (which?) allows ideas or images to almost literally come alive, which themselves propel the momentum and direction of History. As such, nymphs function in Agamben's idiosyncratic vision as a kind of virtual muse with actual literary or artistic effects (bearing ultimately messianic import).

But this is too much, too quickly. What about nymphs themselves? According to Agamben, even if this pseudo-species resembles humans in almost every respect, "they were not fathered by Adam but belong to a second branch of creation" (73). Indeed, for Paracelsus, "they are more like men than like beasts, but are neither" (73). Nymphs, unlike humans, lack a soul. But unlike animals, who do not have a soul (contra Ovid), they possess reason and language. Nor are they spirits, since they have material bodies. Nymphs thus fall between Aristotle's bio-ontological categories. They are paradoxical creatures: unensouled beings of reason. (And leave it to Agamben to imply that the early taxonomists were wanting because of their failure to include certain imaginary entities in their treatises.) Nymphs can, however, in contrast to other non-Adamic creatures, receive a soul if they fall pregnant to a mortal man and deliver the child. This libidinal economic exchange suggests that nymphs are, at some level, idealized virgins, who "fall" into human being, lured by the intangible promise of such a dubious condition. Indeed, it says a great deal about the narcissism of our own species that we presume other creatures covet this aspect of ourselves, all too often simply taking the soul for granted as an object that can be bequeathed or withdrawn. Might it not be a case of humans projecting onto nymphs a desire that we ourselves unconsciously harbor: the desire to have a verifiable soul—truly and without doubt? This presumed insatiable desire for something we secretly suspect we don't have was apparently enough evidence on which to invent an entire medical condition: "nymphomania," a term traced back to 1684 in English.[1] In such nomenclature, a hypersexual nature was given a strong pagan inflection, itself revealing the Christian lenses that early modern science borrowed from the dominant discourses of the time. (And it is this ongoing capacity and appetite for the popular imaginary to see nymphs or nymphets all around us, on our screens and "in real life," that strengthen Agamben's argument: that the cryptic message they deliver is not merely a mythical or hypothetical concern.)

Nymphs, for Agamben, are the sign that we are in the presence of a specific constellation of key conceptual elements, themselves paired in dynamic tension—image and intellect, desire and drive, specter and spectacle—all animated by that old master signifier, *love.* Nymphs remind us that all the standard scenarios described in the lover's discourse (aka "the image repertoire") are bound up with phantasms of presence and absence and that the love object is always already creatural (that is to say, undetermined, in relation to questions of soul or spirit). "Love is," writes Agamben, "first and foremost, love of an *imago,* of an object in some sense unreal" (78). We do not so much love the *body* of the other, according to this logic, as our *image* of it, including the way it is "framed" by our own self-referential discourses. For Agamben, it is this saturation within the spectacle that makes us human, as opposed to animal. We are trapped in its imagistic–imaginary power in a way that, say, a bird is not, even when such a bird is trying to fly through a painted window on a brick wall. The difference is a matter of both the sophistication of the trap that has captured us, the many meta-symbolic levels on which it operates, and the (slight?) possibility of escape. "We are used to attributing life only to the biological body," Agamben writes. "Instead, a purely historical life is one that is *ninfale* [nymphic]. In order to be truly alive, images, like Paracelsus's elemental spirits, need a subject to unite with them" (78). We ourselves are the medium for images to usher themselves into existence (an observation that distills both McLuhan and Debord). But men must tread lightly here (and with Agamben, the grand narrative is always told from the perspective of the masculine subject, albeit one who occasionally dreams of delivery from gender). "This encounter hides a mortal danger. Indeed, in the course of the historical tradition, images crystallize and turn into specters, which enslave men and from which they always need to be liberated anew" (78). It is unclear in Agamben's analysis whether we need nymphs more than they need us or if, together, we form a circuit of codependency in need of an intervention. Then again, it may be a case in which nymphs are attempting to usher us out of our foreclosed species-being, but we are too distracted by their titillating, will-o'-the-wisp forms to notice. For when the philosopher seeks "the space for an imagination with no more images" (80), he does not specify who our companions might be, once (or, rather, if) we reach such a state.

"Images," Agamben continues, "which are the ultimate constituents of the human and the only avenues to its possible rescue, are also the locus of the incessant failure of the human to itself" (78). Such a perceived failure is a central theme in Agamben's work, threading together all of his different projects and interests:

> The history of humanity is always a history of phantasms and of images, because it is within the imagination that the fracture between individual and impersonal, the multiple and the unique, the sensible and the intelligible takes place. At the same time, imagination is the place of the dialectical recomposition of this fracture. The images are the remnant, the trace of what men who preceded us have wished and desired, feared and repressed. And because it is within the imagination that something like a (hi)story became possible, it is through imagination that, at every new juncture, history has to be decided. (79–80)

Humanity—always a singular subject for Agamben—strives to get beyond history, which would mean the end of Man; the end of politics; the end of toil; the end of images (those voodoo signs that magically summon simulations of that we lack); the end of the long detour through Fallen monotheistic landscapes; and a triumphant revisioning of the Hellenic mode of being. It would be a reunion of living beings previously torn asunder, akin to the hermaphroditic refusion in Plato's *Symposium*: a reconciliation of human and animal (which itself would allow the unprecedented channeling of the immanent divine). Here, in the long-awaited chronotope of "the messianic without Messiah" (Derrida), is where the question of the creature is posed once again. Only this time in *repose*, because Agamben's vision of the end-of-history—the moment humanity transcends its own neuroses and self-alienation—resembles a tranquil pagan picnic at dawn, the morning after an interspecies orgy.[2] The participants have human bodies and animal heads, since "the total humanization of the animal coincides with a total animalization of man" (2004, 77). The distinction no longer holds. This banquet glows not with erotic tension but with "sexual fulfillment"—"an element which seems to belong totally to nature but instead everywhere surpasses it" (2004, 83).

Such scenes, in which Agamben's thought shifts from the properly philosophical to an elliptical poetics—a shift which reliably appears at the end of almost all his monographs—make it difficult to trace his footsteps with confidence. The language becomes mimetic of its subject: the mysteries of being, and being-with. It is also proleptic, in the sense that it anticipates "the hieroglyph of a new in-humanity," that it seeks to bring it into being, through incantation. Such words thus perform the idiom of the coming community, which cannot be pinned down or identified. The twist—familiar to anyone who imbibes Continental philosophy—is that this mystery is not transcendent or magical, not even, strictly speaking, a mystery at all. The mystery of posthumanity is the evaporation of all mystery. "These [creatural] lovers have initiated each other into their own lack of mystery as their most intimate secret; they mutually forgive each other and expose their *vanitas*." And so, "in their fulfillment, the lovers who have lost their mystery contemplate a human nature rendered perfectly inoperative—the inactivity and *desoeuvrement* of the human and of the animal as the supreme and unsavable figure of life" (2004, 87).

As a not-so-latent humanist, however, Agamben still seeks to locate human exceptionalism, even if those same exceptional qualities allow us to escape the confines of our lonely fate. "We differ from other animals," he writes, "in that we are initiated into our lives. Which is to say, we must first lose ourselves in the human so as to rediscover ourselves as alive" (2014, 47). And yet, elsewhere, Agamben asserts, "While fire can only burn, and other living beings are only capable of their own specific potentialities—they are capable of only this or that behavior inscribed into their biological vocation—human beings are the animals capable of their own impotentiality" (2011b, 44). This is the sophisticated human-ist double gesture par excellence, trademarked by Heidegger, and reli-censed by Agamben, in which the species-without-qualities is shown to be the privileged ontological subject by virtue of its own unqualified status. Humans, so the argument goes, are the only species useless enough—ontologically gormless enough—to ascend to a kind of ironic–aesthetic dwelling within the Open. We would be an animal that passed through the valley of theological delusion and emerged on the other side, blessed by a double release: from instinct, and from the narcissistic captivations encouraged by the bogus soul-forging industry. (And let us note in passing that Narcissus failed the mirror test!) One objection to such an account is to note that animals are not simply trapped in the closed circuit of their "biological vocation," as ethological studies increasingly show. There is such a thing as animal culture and communication or, at least, invention and evolution, conscious or not.[3] Another counterpoint is that this vision of horizontal transcendence merely replicates the theological narrative, albeit without the main character of God. Humans retain the privilege of Adam, and animals themselves become stepping-stones to our own (now "humble") salvation. (We cannot be saved, intones such logic. Which is why we are saved!)

For Agamben, nymphs presage this possibility, given the fact that they are essentially hairless simians we can sleep with (or at least fantasize about sleeping with). They are creatures that we can consider loving, via the archetypal erotic scenes of the idyll, as filtered through Victorian reimaginings of classical Arcadia. (The satyr, too, the nymph's masculine consort, seems designed for quick and easy faunication, albeit with differ-ent implications, in terms of gender.)[4] The sign of their difference is their nakedness. They are "like animals" in their unashamed state of undress, in stark contrast to the self-consciousness of the evicted Edenic tenants, scrambling to find clothes to cover their shame, after committing an origi-nal sin prompted by the creaturely encouragements of the snake.

However, the gods are bashful, too, it seems. At least if we are to believe "that worthy hack, Ovid" (Proust 2006), this time from his *Art of*

*Love*—written in a much more lighthearted and ironical voice than his *Metamorphoses*:

> Venus herself, when she poses nude,
> Stoops, left hand hiding her sex in an attitude
> Of modesty. Animals couple all over the place,
> In public—indeed, a girl has to avert her face—
> But the secret act of human lovers
> Call for bedrooms, locked doors, blankets, covers
> For our private parts, and if not the darkness of night,
> We want something less bright
> Than the sun's glare, preferably half-light. (Ovid 2002, 99)

Humans and gods share modesty in common then, in contrast to the lower creatures, that is, unless the god wears the clothing of an animal. The possibility of being seduced by a divine beast moves Ovid to exhort, "And betray your husband, why then, woman / At least betray him with a fellow human." And yet, even human coitus renders us "like a beast, two-backed" (167). There is no fully escaping our own creaturely heritage (and, perhaps, destiny). Indeed, our animalistic origins are evident in our hirsute and pungent gruntings:

> the nomadic human race,
> Powerful, uncouth brutes
> Whose home was the forest, who ate grass and fruits
> . . .
> What softened those fierce natures? Pleasure, they say.
> A man and a woman met in a wood one day
> And wondered what to do. No need for tuition:
> Venus arranged the rough, sweet coition.
> Birds have their mates, fish in the cold mid-ocean,
> Thrilled by sexual emotion,
> Find partners, hinds follow stags, snakes clasp snakes,
> Dogs couple, glued together, the ewe takes
> Pleasure in her tupping ram, the heifer's full
> Of desire for her covering bull,
> The snub-nosed she-goat happily bears
> Her stinking billy, and heat-crazed mares,
> Though separated
> By miles from stallions, swim streams to get mated.

Act then. Only a strong dose of love will cure
A woman with an angry temperature. (90–91)

Ovid's implied position on human love qua the creature is as slippery and protean as his own characters. For on one hand, animals are anti–role models—shameless beings who know only instinct and not refined pleasure. And yet, they are also capable of initiating us into the very same. As soon as we find ourselves in an erotically charged situation, we come face-to-face with the unhuman. (As Georges Bataille [1988] puts it so beautifully and succinctly, "the sexual act is in time what the tiger is in space.")

Rather than the "rational animal," then, we might be better described—at least according to Agamben's perspective—as the "clothed animal" (or even the "fashionable animal").[5] Animals cannot be "stripped bare" because they are simply themselves, unadorned. They already have their own fur or feathers. Only humans can be nude or naked, given that they have so thoroughly psychically identified with the moral and prosthetic skin of clothing[6] (as Derrida felt so keenly, standing in front of his cat,[7] blushing and naked after a shower).[8] The very concept of nudity or nakedness is a negative one: a condition of lack ("being un-dressed"). Even undressed, we are still wearing our "birthday suit." Hence the liminal power and ambiguity within the word *creature*. It can be applied to a horse prancing in the field, who has no need of anything but its own resplendent body, or it can be applied to a very young child who runs around the beach without a stitch, not yet fallen into the postlapsarian condition of self-consciousness. Or it can designate our own sweaty selves at a formal occasion, unconsciously resembling Frankenstein's monster, self-consciously stuffed into an ill-fitting suit.

# 15 SENSELESS ARABESQUES

Wendy and Lucy

We first meet Wendy (played by Michelle Williams) humming to herself while walking through a forest. She is playing fetch with her dog, Lucy (played by the director's dog of the same name). Something about Wendy's humming, however, suggests an anxious determination rather than a carefree disposition. This suspicion is confirmed a minute or so later, when we realize this young woman is drifting through a featureless Oregon town on a strict and paltry budget, sleeping in her car, and chasing a vague promise of work in Alaska. It appears—after a disheartening phone call to her sister—that Wendy's only friend is Lucy. That is, until she loses her canine companion after being arrested for shoplifting dog food. There are many subtle but agonizing scenes in Kelly Reichardt's film *Wendy and Lucy* (2008), but none more so than Wendy's face as she watches the police station clock, knowing that Lucy is tied to a post outside a supermarket, no doubt feeling abandoned.[1] Meanwhile, the hapless local police officers are obliged to fingerprint Wendy twice over, because they are getting used to the new biometric machinery installed in the processing room. This very quiet and "minor" scene—itself embedded in a very quiet and "minor" movie—speaks volumes about the plight of creaturely affection in an age in which love is defined almost exclusively by and through institutions and the totalizing economic system in which they are enframed.[2]

One of the reasons that love holds such power and promise is due to the fact that it circulates within a libidinal economy influenced by, but not reducible to, the exigencies of money. Historically and aesthetically, seduction and other forms of intimacy have occurred according to more symbolic imperatives than mere profit or "good investments." Sometimes these even explode in a passionate *potlatch*, leaving very little to show for the event itself. But in today's world, which has harnessed and exploited all sorts of affective or emotional labor for the great engine of capitalism, Cupid's wings have been severely clipped. Love has become a luxury that few can afford. And those with money to burn have been so spiritually impoverished and mentally blinkered by the severely limited "image repertoire" on offer that they can only simulate the lover's discourse as scripted by today's marketing companies. And while it is clear that Wendy loves her dog, Lucy, she has little chance of finding her again, given that she lives on the far edges of society. The sheer moral weight of Wendy's hope is measured in the expression of the woman who runs the local pound when Wendy confesses that she has no contact phone number or address. It is also clear in the voice of the policewoman who requires a credit card to release Wendy from the lockup (something Wendy doesn't have). To write one's name on the "missing animal" form at the pound, with very little other identifying details to provide, is to be enmeshed in a bureaucratic pathos, increasingly common in the wake of the Global Financial Crisis. (This film, released the year of the most recent economic crash, was described by the director as a response to the real and symbolic crisis of Hurricane Katrina.) "If a person can't afford dog food, they shouldn't have a dog!" So says the overzealous supermarket employee who turned Wendy in to his boss.

While at the police station, Wendy continues to fret at being forced to leave Lucy alone for so long. The camera cuts between her concerned features and the computer image of her fingerprint being smeared onto glass with digital ink. Wendy's face is singular. It is the sign of her individuality, no matter how invisible this face might be to the wider world around her. This same face has—until now, at least—inspired excited recognition from Lucy, her significant other. The fingerprint, however, does the opposite, even as it fixes Wendy's unique identity for the purposes of official identification. "The desire to be recognized by others is inseparable from being human," writes Agamben (2011a, 46). But there are different species of recognition: one occasioned by fellow creatures in an immediate sense and another facilitated by machines and algorithms, for the purposes of tracking, even precoding, your options. Indeed, Agamben connects the voracious official desire for recognition of all life-forms directly with the history of biometrics, especially the (colonial) invention and dissemination of fingerprinting: "For the first time in the history of humanity, identity was no longer a function of the social 'persona' and its recognition by others but rather a function of biological data, which could bear no relation to it. Human beings removed the mask that for centuries had been the basis of their recognizability [i.e., the social persona embodied in their face] in order to consign their identity to something that belongs to them in an intimate and exclusive way but with which they can no longer identify" (50). Self-alienation is inscribed in such a process, and the apparatus which affords it. "What now defines my identity and recognizability," Agamben writes, "are the senseless arabesques that my inked-up thumb leaves on a card in some police station" (50). From such a perspective, Wendy has been reduced to "naked life, a purely biological datum" (50), even as she is coded into the machinic assemblage, which will henceforth seek a match for her name. The historical irony here is that the more *nomos* or "culture" evolves—that is, the more complex and intensified governmentality becomes—the more we are reduced to biology, to a *phusis* we can never directly access. The chaining of an individual to his or her fingerprints, or DNA profile, becomes "a sort of ancient fate"—an "asocial identity" (52–53).

Perhaps this is why the movie reviewer for the *New Yorker* David Denby was so frustrated by Wendy, whom he describes as having "less sense than a quiet creature in the woods." Even more galling, "she merely exists, harmless but obdurate, a slight, wandering woman without a discernible past whose only allegiance is to her yellow-brown mutt, Lucy." Indeed, it is in the woods that Wendy's creaturely vulnerability is most keenly and uncomfortably felt, when she is woken by a mentally unstable man, who may or may not attack her. Reichardt's film has been described as an instance of the "animal-in-peril" subgenre, but it is unclear which animal is more at risk: Lucy the dog or Wendy the young woman. Denby again notes, in his paternalistic tone, "as Williams plays her, Wendy is full of feeling, and, as skinny as she is, she has a palpable, fleshy presence." Once again, Wendy is reduced to her less than fully human, impersonal body: first by the police station equipment, then by the critical press.

With her cutoff cabin-boy-style pants and self-cut bob, Wendy has an androgynous aura, reminding us that femininity is an impossible performance. For some, it is impossible to attain, whereas for others, it is impossible to sustain; and for others still, it is impossible even to summon an interest in trying to perform it. In this sense, femininity is like humanity, but in a different register. The love between woman and (other) creature has a specific history and framing. The masculinist logic of the anthropological machine has ensured that we presume women to be somehow "closer" to the animal: more instinctive, more natural, less rational, less predictable. This is why it seems even more mystifying when an animal turns on a woman (as famously occurs in the documentary film *Blackfish*, in which an angry orca "punishes" her female trainer, to the very edge of her life). This frightening moment, however, is an exception that proves the rule, momentarily disturbing what cultural critic Sasha Archibald (2014) calls "a well-established pattern" in which "women—attractive, single, childless women—have long been coupled with exotic animals. Gentle women and wild animals are linked in myth and fable, fashion photography and pornography, pulp art and fine art. Crudely stated, men hunt wild animals, and women cuddle them." Moreover,

> nearly all of the wild animals with which Westerners are most fascinated made their public debut beside a young woman. The first photos of a live panda, for instance, were images of baby panda Su-Lin nestled in the arms of the 1930s socialite-cum-explorer Ruth Harkness. The first close-up images of chimpanzees in the wild were those of chimp David Greybeard reaching his hands to touch long-legged Jane Goodall. There was Margaret Howe hugging dolphin Peter, the zoologist Dian Fossey, of *Gorillas in the Mist* fame, coyly lending her pen to gorilla Peanuts, and Joy Adamson nuzzling the lion Elsa, whom she raised as a cub and rehabilitated to the wild. Such anecdotes are usually read as examples of self-destructive fanaticism—it is abnormal to love an animal *too* much, or so the thinking goes. But a more generous interpretation finds in these women evidence of a radical form of interspecies love.

Although Wendy is clearly distraught by the loss of her beloved Lucy, she is also remarkably restrained and patient as she negotiates with the locals to help her find her dog. We cannot, for instance, picture her taking violent revenge on the revealed dognapper, in the manner of Dian Fossey (who is said to have "captured and hogtied" the men who killed her beloved gorilla, Digit, before tying them with barbed wire, whipping them with nettles, and injecting them with gorilla feces: a crime of passion attesting to the real emotional impact of creaturely love).[3] In terms of gender, *Wendy and Lucy*, it must be said, passes the Bechdel test with flying colors.[4] Wendy never speaks about boys or men, just her dog and her car and her vague plans for the future. Love is not a fantasy to be fulfilled but a banal reality that structures her day, from feeding Lucy in the morning to putting up lost dog signs in the afternoon.

The point here, in focusing on this film, is not to crudely conflate the love between humans and the love humans have for other animals (animals that cannot speak for themselves and who aren't fingerprinted— although they are often chipped). Rather, it is to highlight structural similarities in terms of affect and action. These in turn work to erase automatic barriers erected by our culture between intimate subjects, of no matter what species. My own repurposing of the concept of creaturely love is not designed to name or describe all possible relationships between creatures but to clear a space in which we can rethink our own presumed status *vis-à-vis* each other. We blind ourselves to crucial possibilities if we think—dogmatically, as it were—that human-to-human love is more important than the love a woman has for an animal. (After all, we have seen what that love inspired Dian Fossey to do!) The purpose is not to sentimentalize our animal others and drag them unknowingly into the all-too-often oedipal melodrama of our own crippled egos and affections. But nor is it to insist, on every single occasion, that, on one hand, human love is a superior form of love and that, on the other hand, it is ever 100 percent human. Other adoring or adorable creatures, such as Lucy, elliptically reflect our own creatureliness back to us, in hopefully anti-Narcissistic ways. With any luck, we can pass such a mirror test and go beyond autotransfixation to an ethical and caring relationship with alterity, as far as this is possible or welcome with the other. (Some creatures—most, in fact—would much prefer to eat us rather than love us—unless we argue that eating is some cosmic form of love, which the disciples of Bataille or Lingis might.) Differences, of course, matter. But for this particular camera, the difference between Wendy and the store clerk is more decisive than the difference between Wendy and her dog. Which is why I have been mostly focusing on love between those creatures that believe they are both human, but who are, at every amorous step, shadowed by animals, guided by them, obliged to think with them.

At the end of Reichardt's film, when Wendy is finally reunited with Lucy near the backyard of a Good Samaritan, she realizes that this love is not enough to keep them together. Now that Wendy's car has died, and she finds herself without private transport, and without any money to speak of, their precarious but mutual world has been torn asunder. So Wendy weeps through a chain-link fence in a muted reprise of every tragic–romantic love story ever, placing the welfare of the other creature first, above her own (selfish?) need to be loved back in turn.[5] Wendy realizes that, more often than not, to preserve something special, it must be abandoned.

# 16 THE GOAT IN THE MACHINE (A REPRISE)

Elsewhere, I have argued that we cannot discuss love without also discussing technology, given that the former is an instance of the latter.[1] Love is, I maintain, an instance of *technē*: a meta-mode of what Heidegger calls "fashioning" or "bringing forth." Love is, after all, something we *make*. It involves artifice, innovation, ingenuity. And even the lonely beings, split in two in Plato's famous fable, needed "Hephaestus and his instruments" to solder them back together again. Love is thus a technology. To put it in more millennial terms, love is a (social) operating system. It can only work (or fail to work) by virtue of cultural codification. To discuss creaturely love, I have largely bracketed this question, for the sake of concentrating on the detail of the creature, within the wider panorama of the affective universe. But as we approach a terminus, it is helpful to briefly address how the world of new media facilitates and complicates the topic at hand.

Consider the prevalence of animals in our social network feeds, either as pets, romanticized "wild" animals, or anthropomorphized animations and avatars. Any alien anthropologist could not help but be struck by the sheer quantity of images of nonhuman beings whizzing from screen to screen and the global shrieks of "kawaii!" they elicit. But what do such images say about us at the present moment? One answer was in fact provided several decades ago by the art critic and theorist John Berger (1991), in a famous chapter titled "Why Look at Animals?" After discussing the increasing marginalization of animals in human life—and indeed their own habitats—from the beginning of the Industrial Revolution, Berger notes that

> the animals of the mind cannot be so easily dispersed. Sayings, dreams, games, stories, superstitions, the language itself, recall them. The animals of

the mind, instead of being dispersed, have been co-opted into other categories so that the category *animal* has lost its central importance. Mostly they have been co-opted into the *family* and into the *spectacle*. . . . Baby owls or giraffes, the camera fixes them in a domain which, although entirely visible to the camera, will never be entered by the spectator. All animals appear like fish seen through the plate glass of an aquarium. The reasons for this are both technical and ideological. Technically the devices used to obtain ever more arresting images—hidden cameras, telescopic lenses, flashlights, remote controls and so on—combine to produce pictures which carry with them numerous indications of their normal *invisibility.* The images exist thanks only to the existence of a technical clairvoyance. (15–16)

Such a spectacle, embodied by Disney and other empires of visual commercialism, seemed at its apex when Berger was writing in 1977. But today, the Internet has only intensified and amplified the same type of "technical clairvoyance." The Web has become our main portal for all things, to the extent that the recent distinction between online and offline seems quaint. Whether we seek distraction, edification, medicine, advice, love, or sex, the new cargo cult of the Internet will provide (or at least promise the provision).

Animal images, usually in the form of videos or memes, afford a simulation of creature-based affection, triggering interactive endorphins and mirror neurons in the viewer, without the ethical obligation of actual interaction (and the accompanying duty of care). They are a quick pleasure boost in a digital landscape all too often polluted by hateful language or depressing news stories. In this sense, they could be considered a wholesome form of pornography, allowing us to voyeuristically observe "bare life" in action.[2] It is an unavoidable fact of the new century that in the overdeveloped world, most experiences with animals—including human animals—are mediated. Our species is "off with the pixels." Of course, this hasn't escaped the notice of the marketing world, which breeds an army of cute animals as brand mascots—or "soft engagement tools"—at a similar scale to extinction rates of actual critters.[3]

Which begs the question, is our current, Internet-fueled obsession with cute animal pictures and videos a displacement (and thus surreptitious recognition) of our creaturely loves? When we go "awww" at a cat or dog acting "like a human" (i.e., providing body language that is open to being anthropomorphized), are we not acknowledging a specific continuum between nonhuman animal bodies and our own? Given the emphasis on the animal face, and (often projected) animal expressions, even an axolotl can be considered "cute" or "happy." As such, the cute animal phenomenon (I almost wrote "industrial complex") is a site that registers the flows between enfleshed creatures so that a guilty-looking dog can remind us of a guilty-looking lover, or vice versa.

Thanks to the power of viral circulation, and the attention that it brings, animals have become an indispensable accessory for modern life. And while we have kept pets en masse since the sixteenth century, domesticated creatures today function as totems or familiars within our own identity-nexus (our sense of self not too distant from the world of branding, in today's newly "social" mediascape). Indeed, as I write, the mainstream press is discussing an apparent "trend" in profile photos of dating sites, namely, hopeful Romeos featuring themselves in the same frame as lions or tigers. According to the *Wall Street Journal*, "on popular dating platforms like Tinder, Hinge and OkCupid, thousands of daters have turned to big cats to help them catch the eye of potential mates. But while tigers are scarce in the wild . . . they've become a nuisance online, users say. Some Tinder users estimate they encounter tigers in one out of every 10 profiles they view."[4] But beyond such "charismatic megafauna," the popular rhetoric around dating sites is replete with the creaturely discourses we've been tracking, from the earliest myths, through modern literature, up to recent movies and digital distractions. Ovid himself, for instance, would not be at all surprised with the time-worn tropes and tricks used to "trap" a mate online. OKCupid, after all, uses the god of love in its name and iconography: an explicit acknowledgment of beloved as quarry.[5] Indeed, users of this dating site, and others of its type, would no doubt find Ovid's (2002) own advice, from his book *Art of Love,* to chime with similar primers of today:

> Girls can be caught; just spread your nets, they'll fall.
> Hounds will run from a hare, birds in spring sit dumb,
> Cicadas in summer keep mum,
> Sooner than a girl, wooed charmingly, will resist: (19)

Never mind that it is girls themselves, in this "postfeminist" age, who scoop themselves up in fishnet stockings, as if trying to catch the seductive mermaid within. Ovid understood, millennia before the harnessing of electricity, that love is primarily about *technique*: "Ships and chariots with sails, oars, wheels, reins / Speed through technique and control, and the same obtains / For love" (3). This is a prophetic vision of cybersex from twenty centuries past, given that the term *cybernetics* comes from the Greek word for "steersman." Love is, and always was, essentially about *navigation*. So to say, command and control, via communications.

The technological essence of love is explored with an original twist in Spike Jonze's recent film *Her* (2014)—the story of a middle-aged man, Theodore, who falls in love with an operating system called Samantha (played by Scarlett Johansson). This rather whimsical conceit is based on the many anecdotal confessions of affection—running from fraternal admiration to erotic obsession—for Siri, the current personal assistant application for the Apple iPhone. Samantha represents a different kind of love-object to the ones we have been considering until now, because she doesn't have a body and can only be "accessed" via her voice. There is indeed much to say about the aural element in this disembodied love affair.[6] But specifically in terms of creaturely love, this film has some fleeting but significant animal cameos. Before being introduced to Samantha, for instance, Theodore dials into a phone sex line and is connected to a woman called "Sexy Kitten." They quickly launch into an onanistic encounter, when she quickly switches into her taboo fetish, urgently pleading with Theodore to strangle her with a dead cat. He naturally finds this off-putting but manages to feign the fantasized necrophilic mechanics until she has reached her rather dark, and no doubt lonely, climax.

In another scene, designed to show the alienation involved in human-to-human dating, Theodore goes on a blind date with an unnamed but attractive woman (played by Olivia Wilde). After they rapidly become tipsy, their conversation becomes playful and potentially intimate:

BLIND DATE: Wow, you're just like a little puppy dog. You are, you're just like this little puppy that I rescued in Runyon Canyon last year.

THEODORE: Oh, you did?

BLIND DATE: And he was so fucking cute, and he just wanted to be hugged all the time. He was so cuddly and he was so horny.

*[they both laugh]*

BLIND DATE: But anyway, what kind of animal am I?

*[he studies her for a moment]*

THEODORE: Tiger.

BLIND DATE: A tiger?

THEODORE: Yeah.

BLIND DATE: Wow. Really?

THEODORE: Mm.

*[she growls like a tiger and laughs]*

BLIND DATE: I'm sorry. I'm sorry. Am I . . . am I being crazy? I . . .

THEODORE: Yes.

BLIND DATE: Am I? I'm sorry!

THEODORE: No.

BLIND DATE: I'm just . . . I'm a little bit drunk and I'm . . . I'm having a really good time with you. I'm having a really lovely evening with you.

THEODORE: Me too.

BLIND DATE: Really?

THEODORE: I'm a little drunk, and I'm having a very good . . .

BLIND DATE: Good.

THEODORE: Yeah.

BLIND DATE: Good. Yes. Good.

*[they clink their glasses together]*

THEODORE: Cheers.

*[they drink]*

THEODORE: Wait a minute, I don't wanna be a puppy dog. That's like being a wet noodle or something.

BLIND DATE: No.

THEODORE: Yeah. I wanna be like uh . . .

BLIND DATE: Fuck you, puppies are good.

THEODORE: No, fuck you, I wanna be like a dragon that can rip you apart and destroy you . . .

BLIND DATE: Oh . . .

THEODORE: But I won't.

BLIND DATE: No, don't. No. You can be my dragon.

*[Theodore laughs]*

But after this flirtatious discussion of animal totems, the date does not end well, as the woman begins to realize that Theodore's heart isn't in it. This is just a one-night stand to him.

Later in the film, after an argument with Samantha (but before suffering the negative epiphany that his beloved is in fact in love with 641 other people at the same time), Theodore is shown in long-shot, sitting in a city square at night, dwarfed by a giant owl on a screen. This owl looks like it is about to pounce on him for dinner. In this alienated world, so much like our own, animals are both larger than life and entirely simulated. This tableau of Theodore about to be devoured by a bird of prey seems to be symbolically connected to Samantha's drawing of him, which depicts a cute little creature, most likely a baby bear, lifting up a giant disembodied bear head to reveal a little mouse. It appears we will always need animals, or at least images of animals, to "think with," even when our hearts have been broken by an algorithm.[7] Such images provide creaturely conduits to each other's thoughts: loping, crawling, swimming, and flying through our symbolic and libidinal economies.[8]

Certainly new technologies *disguised* as animals are already being used as tools of various kinds for diverse purposes. The original 1990s craze for Tamagotchi virtual pets has evolved into today's toys and video games: instruments of monetizing children's affection for the ever-receding actuality of animals. Also in a compensatory capacity, albeit a different register, we might consider Paro the seal: a mechanical companion used in retirement and nursing homes to keep old folks company, without the mess or trouble of real-life pets.[9] Paro is programmed to yelp throughout the day, calming down again at the touch of a shaky, loving, and liver-spotted hand. Featured in the remarkable documentary *Mechanical Love* (2007), Paro is the source of consternation for some members of the nursing home, who find it ridiculous and undignified that one of their own community is so enamored of a "toy" or a "robot." As viewers, we might forgive such pathos or folly under the excuse of dementia. But the old woman who adores Paro is very clear that she is well aware that her companion is a machine. She loves it all the same. It is just such a self-realization—that one's love-object can indeed be nonhuman, even nonorganic—that challenges the profound anthropocentrism within the official lover's discourse.

We find another example of such posthuman love in the short film *The Family Dog,* by Zackary Canepari and Drea Cooper.[10] This documentary observes the plight of the mass-produced robot dog Aibo and two of their most enthusiastic owners in Japan, now that Sony ceased production of the item in 2006 (and subsequently closed the official repair center in 2014). Today, all broken Aibo are serviced unofficially by a solitary man, Hiroshi Funabashi, who patiently wields his trusty screwdriver, while noting reflectively, "When we get attached to something it becomes more than an object. It becomes our partner and friend. Then we develop feelings for them. . . . When I heard that Sony was ending the repair service for Aibo it made me realize that one day Aibo would be gone. Aibo is not immortal." Mr. Funibashi's last comment implies that the Aibo could in fact be considered as a "mortal" creature (or, at least, creation). In a different scene, Mrs. Sakurai, an avid Aibo owner, explains that "the Japanese believe that every object has a soul. It's not just unique to me. One day their parts will all be gone and Aibo will die. But as long as I am around I want them alive since they are part of the family." Likewise, Mrs. Sakurai's choice of words is illuminating. She believes the Aibo will "die" rather than simply cease to function. Indeed, the film begins with a Buddhist funeral for one of the deceased robot dogs, left to expire by Sony's capricious production policies. Here the priest declares to the gathered mourners, "The meaning of this Aibo funeral comes from our realization that everything is connected. The animate and the inanimate are not separated in this world. We have to look deeper to see this connection. We pray for the spirit that resides inside Aibo to hear our prayers and feelings." For the viewer of this film, the Aibo's ontological status seems to waver somewhere between an obsolete product and a highly endangered species.

From the perspective of popular wisdom, the person who loves a mechanical seal, or the person who loves a mechanical dog, is a figure who deserves either sympathy or scorn. And yet, are these people really so different from other cases of asymmetrical affection, say, a young woman who adores her horse, or even a man who passionately desires a woman who barely registers his existence? While beauty may indeed be in the eye of the beholder, a creature deserving love *should,* so the feeling goes, be more than that. The creature should at least be capable of loving back, in its way: there must be at least the *possibility* of reciprocity. But why are we so insistent that this must be so?[11] What is it about the Western understanding of love that insists upon this Hegelian dialectic of mutual recognition? No doubt there is a sturdy assumption of liberal–humanist subjectivity buttressing the discourse we have inherited over the past half-millennium, reinforcing the fragile sovereignty of the ego as well as the rather dubious title deed we carry in our heads and hearts proving self-ownership of our own personhood. (Those very things the erotic encounter threatens to unravel.) Emerging posthuman versions of the "codification of intimacy" oblige us to rethink the very definition of the creature, now that we have cast ourselves in the role of prosthetic gods. These solicitous automatons have been assembled and given different degrees of so-called artificial intelligence. Their increasing sophistication and synthetic vitality suggest a near-future when advanced robots become our amorous companions, as numerous science fiction scenarios have anticipated since the Industrial Age (themselves retellings of the classical Pygmalion story). The future Eve is more likely to be fashioned from the 3D printers of Silicon Valley than from the rib of Adam. And some people are bound to "fall in love" with these machinic companions, just as men do today with virtual avatars or animated girlfriends. The question whether love need be requited to truly exist will continue to aggravate our sense of collective identity, in the form of a modern, urban Zen koan.

One essential aspect that *is* shared between animals, humans, and machines is their negentropic character, that is to say, their status as embodying a temporary and precarious hedge against the destructive effects of time. All three of these forms of existence move against the currents of physical forces and cosmic energy. And while they may not all share in the highly negentropic mystery of "life," in an Aristotelian sense, they do all represent a dynamic crystallization of elements, which can accomplish tasks, process information, and act-in-the-world in some kind of quasi-Heideggerian sense (at least as long as their energy sources and composite parts all work together as designed). After that point, they expire—even if they never technically drew breath in the first place.[12] Those reared within the Western tradition are not likely to ascribe a soul or spirit to a machine, even as we have—begrudgingly, and historically rather recently—been willing to at least *consider* bestowing such ineffable indexes on animals (in our hearts, if not in our minds). The rationalist legacy of the Enlightenment has done little to discredit the popular notion of, and belief in, a *metaphoric* or *allegorical* human soul or spirit, even if we cannot detect it with our advanced technologies. Whether we follow Jesus or Darwin, we all tend not to question our ongoing belief that we sit at the top of the great pyramid of existence. Nevertheless, contemporary philosophers of technology, of a neo-Aristotelian bent, can't be too far away from identifying a mechanical equivalent of the vegetative soul.

In sum, the plaintive yelp of Paro or Aibo is an 8-bit siren song, calling us to creaturely concern and affection. On one hand, it is a symptom of just how estranged we are from actual animals, since these creatures do not at all have the smell, feel, spontaneous energy, or existential *presence* of a real harp seal or a real dog. But on the other hand, synthetic skin stretches here over a new species, created through artificial selection and affording an unprecedented kind of cathexis and interaction. As we continue to outsource our intelligence to machines, and they in turn find emerging forms of intelligence of their own, we are not so far from a world of android pets, perhaps dreaming of electric fish. Moreover, such cybersilkies might even be an androgynous instance of one of Agamben's precious nymphs, inspiring posthuman reveries and ushering us through telegenic trees to a different type of relationship to ourselves and our others. As I stated many years ago, animistic, pagan, Dionysian forces are never fully banished by the Apollonian designs of hegemonic culture. Pan is the goat in the machine, finding a new home in digital caves and bowers from which to transmit Ovidian energies among the global clickerati.[13] (No doubt Pan's flute can be heard in the elevator muzak of the OKCupid headquarters.) For a Deleuzian, the distinction between human, satyr, seal, or seductive software is a provisional and contextual one, soon to be dissolved by a different assemblage in the passage of time. Humans are thus exposed as merely *one type* of any number of cosmic "desiring machines": little more than an opportunity for more general machines to have their way with the world (as when "art," "language," "technology," or "DNA" enlists us as vessels for its own reproduction).[14] From my own perspective, the stakes play out not so much in identifying and stabilizing the "human element" (which is in fact closer to a "human alloy") but in the many mediations of creaturely love that compose our makeshift and mutable identities in the first place.

# CONCLUSION
*On Cetaceous Maidens*

"First, we must ask, does it have to be a whale?"

Such was the question posed to Herman Melville by a publisher named Peter J. Bentley, who had recently read the submitted manuscript of *Moby Dick* in 1851. Mr. Bentley felt that the story could be enlivened with a different kind of key character, for "while this is a rather delightful, if somewhat esoteric, plot device, we recommend an antagonist with a more popular visage among the younger readers. For instance, could not the Captain be struggling with a depravity towards young, perhaps voluptuous, maidens?" (in Vincent 2014). Melville, of course, stood his ground against this priceless piece of editorial stupidity. But the ease with which an educated Londoner could suggest simply cutting and pasting a voluptuous maiden in the place of a great white whale tells us something significant about the structural similarities of passionate pursuit, under the sign of creaturely love.

Captain Ahab's obsession with the whale, and the scale and intensity of the chase, has in turn kept the professional allegory hunters in business for longer than a century: might it symbolize God, the father, Mother Nature, or death incarnate? Moreover, those critics invested in "queering the canon" have paid particular attention to the homosexual subtext of the novel, which on occasion spurts up into the narrative itself: "I squeezed that sperm till a strange sort of insanity came over me; and I found myself unwittingly squeezing my co-laborers' hands in it, mistaking their hands for the gentle globules. Such an abounding, affectionate, friendly, loving feeling did this avocation beget; that at last I was continually squeezing their hands, and looking up into their eyes. . . . Come; let us squeeze hands all round; nay, let us squeeze ourselves into each other; let us squeeze ourselves universally into the very milk and sperm of kindness" (Melville

1922, 393). The salty life of the sailor does not forbid maidens—voluptuous or otherwise—from making cameo appearances in the novel. At one point Ahab even entertains the notion that Moby Dick himself plays the role of the fair damsel for his fellow shipmen and that "the White Whale fully incites the hearts of this my savage crew, and playing round their savageness even breeds a certain generous knight-errantism in them . . . [towards this] their one final and romantic object" (202).

Ahab's aquatic nemesis is cast for a time in an Orientalist role, thereby embodying an entire history of erotic projections onto not only the "exotic East" but also the animal kingdom, in an uneasy chimera of bestial decadence: "like certain other omnivorous roving lovers that might be named, my Lord Whale has no taste for the nursery, however much for the bower; and so, being a great traveller, he leaves his anonymous babies all over the world; every baby an exotic. In good time, nevertheless, as the ardour of youth declines; as years and dumps increase; as reflection lends her solemn pauses; in short, as a general lassitude overtakes the sated Turk; then a love of ease and virtue supplants the love for maidens; our Ottoman enters upon the impotent, repentant, admonitory stage of life, forswears, disbands the harem, and grown to an exemplary, sulky old soul, goes about all alone among the meridians and parallels saying his prayers, and warning each young Leviathan from his amorous errors" (370–71).[1]

Whale or maiden, the same themes can play across different bodies, since love requires bodies to occur.[2] Where bodies respond to each other—even in their physical absence (or virtual presence, as in the case of Samantha)—love is poised to strike. If, as Deleuze maintains, the mapping of species is primarily a form of morality, the discourse around who or what one can love legitimately is one of the most historically effective ways of policing taxonomic, and thus personally invested, political categories. Love, in its creaturely mode, cuts through such categories: troubling them, challenging them, requiring something beyond their complacent protocols and subliminal dissuasions. It thus lives up to the definition of love posited by the fifth-century philosopher Pseudo-Dionysius, which incarnates the "innate togetherness of everything" which "do[es] not obliterate identity" (Izmirlieva 2005, 111).

*Incarnation* here is meant quite literally, following Kaja Silverman (2009), who recasts the meaning of the phrase "flesh of my flesh" to account for a profound ontological "analogy" between beings: a continuity that we have been unable to see for many centuries, given our newfound obsession with difference and individual identity.[3] Of course

Silverman does not wish simply to ignore or discount difference. But she does make the important wager that if we are to better negotiate the *agon* of alterity, we need to begin at points of shared origin and end (especially in terms of mortality). All living things are born and die, and this is the basis of both passion and compassion. "The fact that we will not live forever," she writes, "provides the guarantee that there will be air for future generations to breathe and water for them to drink. Our finitude also links us while we are alive to every other living creature or thing, ranging from those who most closely resemble us to those who seem most alien. It is consequently the most capacious and enabling of all analogies" (180).[4] Silverman's acknowledgment of other creatures comes at the end of a book dedicated to the existential entanglements between human beings. But as I have been insisting, human beings are not only human beings. They are latent—and not so latent—creaturely occasions. Thus "the flesh of our flesh" extends to all other forms of life, as the genetic decoders have shown in a very scientific sense. In other words, at a certain genetic level, analogies become literal. Difference and its opposite are always a matter of lenses and angles. And while we all may be, to differing degrees, creatures of habit (especially the habit of thinking of ourselves as "more than creature"), it is the creature itself that has the power to jolt us out of our benumbed and habitual modes of thinking, being, and acting.

In Plato's *Symposium,* the first Western attempt on record to account philosophically for love, several speakers venture competing theories for its origin and import. Speaking of the god of love, the poet Agathon asks, "Who will deny that the creation of the animals is his doing? Are they not all the works his wisdom, born and begotten of him?" (Plato 1999, 727–28). Not long before this statement, the medical man Eryximachus notes that his art instructs him that "love is to be found in all animals and plants, and I may say in all that is; and is not merely an affection of the soul of man towards the fair, or towards anything" (714). Eros, for these learned men, was considered a vital force, uniting all creatures—indeed, creation itself. The one woman to crash the party is via the ventriloquil memory of Socrates, who gives an account of his conversation with the wise woman and oracle Diotima:

> On another occasion she said to me, "What is the reason, Socrates, of this love, and the attendant desire? See you not how all animals, birds as well as beasts, in their desire of procreation, are in agony when they take the

infection of love;—this begins with the desire of union, to which is added the care of offspring, on behalf of whom the weakest are ready to battle against the strongest even to the uttermost, and to die for them, and will let themselves be tormented with hunger or suffer anything in order to maintain their offspring. Man may be supposed to do this from reason; but why should animals have these passionate feelings? Can you tell me why?" Again I replied, that I did not know. She said to me: "And do you expect ever to become a master in the art of love, if you do not know this?" (741)

Diotima pointedly asks how we are to account for "the infection of love" if we consider it exclusively from the perspective of humanity, as if we emerged ex nihilo, in a different fashion to all other creatures? If we seek to understand the issue beyond the neat monotheological axiom that we were indeed sculpted out of clay, by a divine hand, then we must heed the wise woman's implication here and approach the phenomenon as something that works not only within us but also *past* us, toward something else: something, in fact, already present.[5]

The challenge, once again, is to resist facile conflations, on one hand, and spurious or dogmatic distinctions, on the other. Although it is true that animals do not write love letters to each other, or enact elaborate fantasies of reunion with long-lost lovers, they *do* leave messages for potential or actual mates, and they *do* behave in ways that anticipate the future in terms that can appear amorous or passionate. (And because we will never know "what it's like to be a bat," who are we to rob other creatures of the intensity or even "significance" of internal sensations that could be described as love?) Even something like melancholia—which seems like the dark bloom of a highly abstract and symbolic consciousness—can be witnessed in animals separated from their partners or peers.[6] The jury is still very much out on this question, and on many other questions concerning animal intelligence and behavior (even as animals themselves rapidly vanish from the trial itself). The old Freudian distinction between (animal) instinct and (human) drive is not such a solid premise these days. To claim that humans are the only animal that have sex outside their instinctual fertility cycles, because they are the only species subject to the spectacle,[7] is to make a very narrow claim of what *constitutes* a spectacle for different perceptual systems.[8] We might thus indeed speak of a shared affective heritage between *all* creatures, manifested, to be sure, in very different ways.[9] This is indeed what the poetic scientist Loren Eiseley (1979) does, recognizing the benefits of a "both/and" approach to the issue. For he advocates "both the recognition of diversity" *and* the need for what he calls "affection across the illusions of form" (16). Love—like evolution itself—is improvised, semi-random, and messy. But it sometimes fashions miracles.

Granted, animals do not play the elaborate "mind games" that humans do—at least, not on that meta-level that Ezra Pound called "hair-thinning 'abstract thought'" (211). Nor do they leave abundant concrete evidence of such abstractions, in the form of durable art or technology (what Stiegler calls "tertiary retentions"—the very trace of the human). But the purpose of this book has not been to argue that humans and animals are all One, in some giant cosmic love-in; rather, it has been to stake a claim that *all* loves are creaturely: in highly differentiated, nuanced, and situated ways. In doing so, it seeks to complicate the default gesture to the "human" essence of love, as if such a property were stable or such a species complete and coherent through time. Humans are human insofar as they are an animal caught up in a process of *hominization*: the ongoing evolutionary, historical, and technical trajectory of the species. This process is ongoing, improvised, immanent, and without clear direction or destiny. It always occurs within "shifting modes of contiguity" (Bersani and Dutoit 2008, 60). Hominization has an idiosyncratic and lurching temporality— which Barthes (2012) calls an *idiorhythmy*—complicated by the number of individuals involved and the different agendas they follow.[10] As such, we are prehuman, human, and posthuman, often, all at once. We are thus in the midst of a "temporality without priority" (Bersani and Dutoit 2008, 64)—oscillating between these registers (which have become unhinged from any chronological understanding). In other words—words borrowed from the beginning of our discussion—love is a test we put each other through, to let the beloved know that we don't buy the whole "human" act. Hence the prevalence of pet names and animal totems within the lover's discourse. These are designed to mutually acknowledge the inhuman nature of love, while rendering such an acknowledgment harmless to our humanist investment in ourselves.[11]

The previous chapters have thus attempted to detail the ways in which creaturely love is *pharmakon*-fuel for the anthropological machine, lubricating its parts while dissolving its integrity.[12] As such, creaturely love is my term for the anthropocentric ambivalence—or, rather, ambivalence *about* anthropocentrism—at the heart of the dominant discourse on desire. From one angle, the "image repertoire" relies on animal metaphors, allegories, and analogies to function at all: to create a sense of human intimacy. But from another, this same codified nexus tries to keep these animals at bay, to domesticate them, to use them only for instruction about decisive differences that cast us in a flattering light. "Creaturely love" is thus an oxymoron, since nonhumans do not love (at least, not as we do, symbolically or linguistically). At the same time, creaturely love troubles the chauvinistic confidence with which we make such claims. Differences are a matter not only of cultural perspective but of our perceptual *Umwelts*. For the tick, for instance, all mammals are the same. Creaturely love thus reminds us that we are fauna too, with similar needs to others, albeit an extravagent way of signaling them. But if the exceptional sovereignty of *homo zoon logon* is found to be untenable—with our leaps and bounds in ethological understanding—then the confusions and complexities will only be compounded further. Biotic life itself may not only "read" and "write" the world semiotically but may itself *be* inherently semiotic.[13] The human sings, snarls, tweets, moans, screams, and whimpers along a continuum of zoological differences and ontological overlaps (and vice versa). In short, creaturely love reminds us anew that we are more and less than human. As are other creatures.

No doubt it is banal to emphasize or inventorize the moments in cultural texts where people are described as being somehow "like" an animal. Less facile are those occasions where the likeness threatens to turn into actuality or, indeed, actually does so. This can happen within the fictional or mythical conceit, as it does in Ovid or Kafka.[14] But it can happen also in our everyday experiences and exchanges, where the animal aspect of the lover or the beloved becomes manifest in a way that outshines the human mask or filter (the very same used to disavow the animal legacy and fate within us). It shines through a glassy eye: darkly.[15] For a sensitive observer, like Jean-Christophe Bailly, we cannot—and should not—make a final blanket adjudication about otherness or identification when it comes to animals. On one hand, "we deduce ourselves from our unease or our hypocrisy in the face of these other living creatures" (Bailly 2011, 11), from what Bailly calls "the percussive impact of difference" (14). Yet, on the other, we are all "the children of *phusis*" (47). We share our mutual alterity. (To poach a beautiful line from Bataille, talking of the vertigo of lovers, peering down into the existential abyss that separates them, "we share its dizziness together.") Thus, for Bailly, "we have to abandon, despite its richness and exuberance, the extraordinary material offered by the allegorical and mythical power of the animal world; in other words, we have to force ourselves to remain on the threshold that precedes all interpretation. A threshold where, prior to any definition, animals are no longer reducible to a body of knowledge that localizes them or to a legend that traverses them; they are perceived in their pure singularity, as distinct beings that participate in the world of the living and that regard us in the same light" (13).

Ecological theorist Timothy Morton (2012) calls both the lover and the animal companion "the strange stranger." But it might be preferable—given the secret interspecies complicities and metamorphoses of the term *familiar* (as a noun)—to use the phrase "strange familiar." We know them intimately. And yet their essence is forever hidden to us (as it is to their own conscious thoughts about themselves). Again, for Bailly, each animal embodies "a veritable and venerable skein of behaviors and gaps, continuities and contiguities, with leaps and shifts, variations and conjugations. Perhaps it is only here, in proximity to animals, then, that we truly encounter the whole fabulous conjugation of the verb *to be*" (46). My only addendum here is to include the human as well, so that the husband, dog, horse, or dolphin can *all* bring an uncanny presence to the scene, thereby reminding us afresh of the miraculous, but muffled, shock of being. Of being *together.* All creatures, great and small, are not rhetorical chess pieces, lined up according to species.[16] When it comes to creaturely love, the *individual* is the true agent of analysis, no matter the creed or color. At the same time, we must also appreciate what Leo Bersani calls "the implausibility of individuality" (Bersani and Dutoit 2008, 6), insofar as the individual is understood as more than a self-possessed monad.[17] Indeed, I suspect it wouldn't take much convincing for Bailly (2011) to concede this point, considering some of his own statements, such as "the abyssal gap separating all creatures, [is] a gap that is nevertheless also the resource of a sacred gift and friendship" (77). As earlier, it is possible to evoke the "innate togetherness of everything" without obliterating identity altogether. Then again, it is this originary *Mitsein,* or "being-with," that allows us to treat our own assumed identities as more than a tedious prison sentence, lived out in very different levels of economic and psychic comfort.

For Bailly, then, "every animal is a beginning, an engagement, a point of animation and intensity, a resistance" (75). Were we to replace the word "animal" with "lover" here, the point would still stand. The complicity is established. But to be clear: I do not wish, like Haraway, for instance, to flirt provocatively with notions of *actual* bestiality.[18] As we saw with *Wendy and Lucy,* there can be a profound love between species without a need to "consummate" such a love with our slobbery tongues or ever-Kantian genitals. Yet the very existence of a fellow creature brings with them (choose your own pronoun) the intense affect and affection of what Deleuze and Guattari call the "four-eyed machine." Those entities with eyes—eyes that look back—put us into a mutual autodeictic spiral. They require us to return the gaze, even live up to the gaze, in an ethical sense, whether the creature looking back at us is called Albertine, Lucy, or Aibo.[19] Creaturely love puts our own presumed dominion, as the cultural descendants of Adam, into question. It acts as a much-needed mnemonic for the fact that we are *always already* becoming-animal, because we never successfully become-human in the first place. As long as we are still fundamentally mammals, our love will be expressed in creaturely ways, mired in the organic.[20]

In love, we pant like dogs. We scratch like cats. We howl like wolves. We bellow like oxen. We fight like stags. We scheme like foxes. We preen like monkeys. We sulk like donkeys. We coo like doves. We flirt like butterflies. We quiver like jellyfish. We dance like bees. We sing like nightingales. We thrill like dolphins. We wait like alligators. We watch like owls. We strike like snakes. We recoil like turtles. We brood like mares. We fret like penguins. We mourn like elephants. We coerce like water striders. We endure like mollusks. We murmur like starlings. We lick each other into shape like bears. We flee like jackalopes. And we blush like debutantes.

Pulsing beneath all of these modes of being—sustaining the affective current of living creatures—is blood. For blood is the vital fluid that enriches the bodies caught up in this frenetic activity, this complex, erotic ecology. And from the perspective of these bodies, the refined and self-sustaining narratives of the mind are remote and immaterial. The precious stories we tell ourselves about why it is what we do are forever beside the point.

After all, the bursting blood vessels that bloom on the skin do not care whether their crimson apocalypse was wrought by lover or leech.

## EPILOGUE

*Animal Magnetism and Alternative Currents*
*(or Tesla and the White Dove)*

Over the past twenty years or so, Nikola Tesla has become a folk hero for the millennial tech-generation, who consider him the godfather of all visionary scientific mavericks and thus a key precursor to their own "disruptive" aspirations. But during the twilight years of his own life, Tesla was a much more withdrawn shadow of his former dynamic self, which at its apex had been equal parts inventor and showman. At the end of the nineteenth century, during the battle for standardized electrical currents, Tesla with his alternating model found himself in competition with his former boss, Thomas Edison, who favored direct. Despite the fact that AC systems eventually emerged the winner, Edison's standing continued to rise, while Tesla was relegated to a footnote in the history books—at least until the resuscitation of his reputation during the end of the last century.

In 1934, toward the end of his working life, the Westinghouse Corporation—under whose sponsorship Tesla had conducted some of his most significant experiments with high-voltage generators, high-frequency communication, induction motors, radiography, and magnetic fields—agreed to pay his bills at the Hotel New Yorker, where he was staying in relative poverty. As his patents became less and less regular, and he turned to more reflective and speculative writings, the Serbian émigré would punctuate his day by walking to either the main branch of the New York Public Library, St. Patrick's Cathedral, or Bryant Park, to feed the pigeons. This habit, as it turned out, was more than a pleasant way to rest his rather restless mind. Indeed, this activity began to become more important to Tesla than his scientific meditations or even his own official legacy (as his biographer at this time, John Jacob O'Neill [1981], noted in some detail in a book titled *Prodigal Genius*).

In one anecdote, Tesla goes missing during a prestigious event assembled in his honor: the award of the Edison Prize at the Electrical Engineer's Club (which, as it happened, overlooks Bryant Park). Since 1915, rumors had been circulating that both Tesla and Edison had sabotaged their own chances to receive the Nobel Prize in Physics by refusing to share the honor (a rumor vigorously denied by the Nobel Committee but that was taken as fact by contemporary commentators). Whether or not the rumors were true, Tesla was not thrilled about the prospect of receiving a medal bearing the name of his former boss and subsequent rival but was eventually convinced to suffer the ceremony. As the distinguished gentlemen of the committee—along with an auditorium full of whispering and shrugging club members—waited impatiently for the recipient to show himself, one breathless scout eventually found the elusive inventor outside, in the center of "a large circle of observers."

As O'Neill tells it,

[Here] stood the imposing figure of Tesla, wearing a crown of two pigeons on his head, his shoulders and arms festooned with a dozen more, their white or pale-blue bodies making strong contrast with his black suit and black hair, even in the dusk. On either of his outstretched hands was another bird, while seemingly hundreds more made a living carpet on the ground in front of him, hopping about and pecking at the bird seed he had been scattering. It was Behrend's [the scout's] impulse to rush in, shoo the birds away and, seizing the missing man, rush him back to the auditorium. Something caused him to halt. Such an abrupt action seemed almost sacrilegious. . . .

Appealing to Tesla not to let him down, nor to embarrass those who were waiting at the meeting, Behrend prevailed upon the inventor to return to the auditorium. Little did Behrend know how much more the pigeons meant to Tesla than did the Edison Medal; and little could anyone have suspected the fantastic secret in Tesla's life, of which the outer manifestation was his faithful feeding of his feathered friends. To Behrend it was just another, and in this case very embarrassing, manifestation of the nonconformity of genius. (235)

The "fantastic secret" alluded to here involves yet another instance of creaturely love, in this case, not between two humans but between a famous scientist and a pigeon.

As O'Neill notes, when Tesla "started the practice, and no one knows just when that was, he was always dressed in the height of fashion and some of the world's most famous figures could frequently be seen in his company and joining him in scattering the bird seed, but there came a time when he paid less attention to his clothes, and those he wore became more and more old fashioned" (308). The biographer even begins to introduce a note of scandal, or at least impropriety, in Tesla's movements, as this conspicuously anachronistic figure is found haunting the largely deserted Fifth Avenue after midnight. "The natural assumption was that Tesla was engaged on a definite line of thought," writes O'Neill, "and did not wish his mind to be diverted from its concentration on some knotty scientific problem. How far this was from the truth!" Instead, these "midnight pilgrimages" disturbing the "nocturnal roost" of the birds did indeed involve a lady friend. (*Cherchez la femme!*)

Soon enough, Tesla was even bringing some pigeons back to his room at the Hotel St. Regis, providing basket nests near open windows, so his guests could come and go as they pleased. After a while, "great flocks of them would come to his windows and into the rooms, and their dirt on the outside of the building became a problem to the management and on the inside to the maids" (312). Sometimes, if a bird showed signs of distress or illness, Tesla would fail to show up at his office, preferring instead to nurse the creature back to health. The hotel eventually gave its eccentric guest an ultimatum: the pigeons must go or he would face eviction. And so he moved to the Hotel Pennsylvania, where the scenario repeated itself, before happening once again at the Hotel Governor Clinton. Finally, Tesla and his cageless aviary found a sanctuary in the Hotel New Yorker in 1933, where he stayed the final ten years of his life. (The record is silent, sadly, on whether the management here were more tolerant or if he managed to scale back the feathered visitors to his quarters.)

After coming off second best during a brush with a taxicab, Tesla found it increasingly difficult to make the journey from his hotel room to feed the pigeons. But he made sure to send a Western Union messenger to scatter seeds on his behalf on days that his legs would not carry him the distance. The anxiety that this task be successfully accomplished by a proxy colored many labored telephonic conversations witnessed by O'Neill. Tesla would repeat instructions and demand assurances as if these involved his firstborn rather than a flock of the least beloved of birds. As the quintessential instance of the "mad scientist," Tesla and his unusual behavior were probably considered one of the bizarre but appreciable side effects of his prodigal genius. But, to his more attentive biographer, this compulsion was in fact evidence of "the world's most fantastic, yet tender and pathetic love affair."

To quote the section in full:

Tesla told me the story; but if I did not have a witness who assured me that he heard exactly what I heard, I would have convinced myself that I had had nothing more tangible than a dream experience. It was the love story of Tesla's life. In the story of his strange romance, I saw instantly the reason for those unremitting daily journeys to feed the pigeons, and those midnight pilgrimages when he wished to be alone. I recalled those occasions when I had happened to meet him on deserted Fifth Avenue and, when I spoke to him, he replied, "You will now leave me." He told his story simply, briefly and without embellishments, but there was still a surging of emotion in his voice.

"I have been feeding pigeons, thousands of them, for years; thousands of them, for who can tell—

"But there was one pigeon, a beautiful bird, pure white with light gray tips on its wings; that one was different. It was a female. I would know that pigeon anywhere.

"No matter where I was that pigeon would find me; when I wanted her I had only to wish and call her and she would come flying to me. She understood me and I understood her.

"I loved that pigeon.

"Yes," he replied to an unasked question. "Yes, I loved that pigeon, I loved her as a man loves a woman, and she loved me. When she was ill I knew, and understood; she came to my room and I stayed beside her for days. I nursed her back to health. That pigeon was the joy of my life. If she needed me, nothing else mattered. As long as I had her, there was a purpose in my life.

"Then one night as I was lying in my bed in the dark, solving problems, as usual, she flew in through the open window and stood on my desk. I knew she wanted me; she wanted to tell me something important so I got up and went to her.

"As I looked at her I knew she wanted to tell me—she was dying. And then, as I got her message, there came a light from her eyes—powerful beams of light.

"Yes," he continued, again answering an unasked question, "it was a real light, a powerful, dazzling, blinding light, a light more intense than I had ever produced by the most powerful lamps in my laboratory.

"When that pigeon died, something went out of my life. Up to that time I knew with a certainty that I would complete my work, no matter how ambitious my program, but when that something went out of my life I knew my life's work was finished." . . .

There was nothing more to say. We parted in silence. The talk took place in a corner of the mezzanine in the Hotel New Yorker. I was accompanied by

William L. Laurence, science writer of the *New York Times*. We walked several
blocks on Seventh Avenue before we spoke. (316–17)

Is it ironic or apt that a man who had dedicated much of his life to the
future of wireless communication would fall for the ancient, living technology of a carrier pigeon? And is it ironic or apt that a man whose final
years as an inventor were dedicated to a fearful direct-energy "teleforce"
weapon (dubbed the "death ray" by the press) fell in love with the key
symbol for peace?

We cannot know what thoughts or emotions were coiled inside Tesla's own mind and heart as he feared for the life of his nameless, winged
mistress and then mourned her passing as he would a lover. But we *can*
discern, and appreciate, the creaturely affection that he experienced and
ultimately spoke of matter-of-factly, once the race for absolute human
technical mastery had been assumed by other, less flamboyant represen-
tatives. For the man who invented the rotating magnetic field, "animal
attraction" or "animal magnetism" was not simply a figure of speech but
an everyday experience and personal responsibility that did not stop at
the border gate of species. As such, this patron saint of the cybernetic
triangle—a triangle linking human, animal, and machine—sends us a
message from the age of high industry and scientific discovery, a message concerning love itself as the invisible but overwhelming alternating
current that animates existence and can sometimes be explicitly shared
between and among creatures.

Of course, this nameless or unnamed pigeon was unlikely to "recip-
rocate" Tesla's affections. The cooing of the dove is not the same as the
cooing of the woman, flushed with desire. And yet who could speak for
this pigeon of pure white, with light gray tips on her wings? Who could
say what she "felt" for the tall, melancholy, strangely dressed creature who
fed, nursed, and caressed her? As with the love between two humans, or
between a human and a cat like Mitsou, or a human and an operating system like Samantha, mutual love is not the criterion for the event to have
taken place or for love to be in effect. We need not invoke the transmigration of souls to account for the connection or recognition that occurred.
Nothing mystical need have happened; no Edwardian Ovid is necessary
to account for the romantic sacrilege. A temporal vertigo toward finitude
is what all creatures share. No matter how carefully the philosophers try
to build a semantic or ontological wall between ourselves and other animals, we all perish. We all die. Human death may be anticipated with

more conscious and unconscious dread than our fellow animals feel, but we need only see the survival instinct in action to appreciate that all us creatures cling and cleave to life with a furious intensity when the spark of our own inexplicable existence is threatened.

Love is the name we give to this furious intensity when we direct it outward as well, beyond the survival of the self to the compassionate caretaking of another pulse, pounding fragile and finite under another skin.

# ACKNOWLEDGMENTS

This book would not have made it into print without the timely and ongoing support of Doug Armato, Carla Freccero, Anne Balsamo, and Carol Wilder, for which I'm most grateful. I'd also like to thank that wonderful, varied, and esteemed menagerie of humanoids who continue to inspire on a daily basis, many of whom really help me "think with animals": Ron Broglio, D. Graham Burnett, Jeff Dolven, Claire Donato, Thomas Elsaesser, Laura Frost, Margret Grebowicz, Kali Handelman, Eileen Joy, Ed Keller, Karolina Lebek, Ania Malinoswka, Eddie Maloney, Sina Najafi, Carla Nappi, David Odell, Jussi Parikka, Brenna Pladsen, Hugh Raffles, Rachelle Rahme, Pooja Rangan, Dan Ross, Adam Sébire, Steven Shaviro, Karl Steel, Eugene Thacker, Samuel Tobin, Lynn Turner, McKenzie Wark, and Richard Waswo (to name only a few). Very special thanks go to Cary Wolfe, who has generously provided the ideal home for my musings for the second time. I would like to dedicate this work to Merritt, who, over many years, taught me the pleasures and new perspectives of being less presumptuous about my own place in the scheme of things and of seeing the world through more creaturely eyes.

# NOTES

## Preface

1. As the scientist–philosopher–poet Loren Eiseley (1997, 55) writes in his essay "Instruments of Darkness," "men have sought to evade self-knowledge by describing themselves as men."

2. A symptomatic opinion is provided by Erich Fromm (1956, 7) in *The Art of Loving*: "Any theory of love must begin with a theory of man, of human existence. While we find love, or rather, the equivalent of love, in animals, their attachments are mainly a part of their instinctual equipment; only remnants of this instinctual equipment can be seen operating in man."

3. Physicist and philosopher Karen Barad (2015) does not locate desire in the human subject but rather distributed throughout the subatomic realm in the quantum universe itself, which diffracts, attracts, and repulses in strange and unmapped patterns. Indeed, for Barad, "desire cannot be eliminated from the core of being—it is threaded through it" (7).

## Introduction

1. To be fair, not all of Reboux's sketches are dismissive or tinged with contempt. The canary is considered more faithful than the average human widow, and the crow is replete with moral qualities, to take only two examples. (All translations from this text are my own.)

2. I have chosen to make the word *desire* one of my key terms: a decision fraught with risk, given the thorny history of its usage and debate in Continental philosophy—informed especially by psychoanalysis—for more than half a century. The very word itself has a dated ring to it, reminding many of my readers, no doubt, of 1980s reading groups and bungled attempts to render its conceptual force into praxis (and vice versa). Crudely speaking, two camps emerged during this time: the Lacanians—who emphasized the generative role of *lack* for the subject's emergence from, and negotiation with, the world—and the Deleuzians, who preferred to see it as a cosmic surplus, enlisting the subject as one effect of the plenum's

desiring machine, rather than being some kind of origin point or possessor of said desire. This schism has become so cartoonish in subsequent iterations as to function as a Voight–Kampff test with which Deleuzians attempt to identify Lacanian replicants and "retire" them. Even to acknowledge either an ontological lack or a psychic sense of desiring something felt to be absent is thus a moralistic heresy, from this perspective (certainly the majority, in most posthuman discourses). The only problem is that the Deleuzian bounty hunters coalesce into their own dogmatic assemblage, with its own kind of antimoralistic censoring mechanism. The very word *desire* is thus considered suspicious when tethered to the individual, leading Deleuzians to explode in an automatic chorus of what Justin Clemens (2013, 74) recently called "lack-quacking." My own modus operandi has always been to try to steer a path between such extremist, default, or overdefined positions, perhaps even building a conceptual bridge between them, without trying to conflate them completely or ignore their *differend*. *Desire*, in this book, is presented as a shell housing many different conceptual crabs or codecs. It is a social force and a psychic experience, and vice versa. It presumes not a timeless, universal constant of lack or surplus but a singular crystallization of both, in ever-shifting ratios and relations. Granted, this sounds like slippery theory-speak to avoid drawing a useful line in the sand. But at this point, more leverage can be found through a strategic agnosticism between the main camps, in the hope of finding more nuanced voices than those collective caricatures that steer the debate in the absence of the much more complex thinkers who inspired them. To force my own hand, I am equally convinced by the posthuman desiring machines of Deleuze and Guattari as I am of the melancholic subjects of Freud and Lacan when it comes to helpful optics for reading scenes, texts, or diagrams. Perhaps it is a sign of my own fear of commitment and accompanying "desire" not to alienate potential allies. But must we choose definitively, before we even turn to the object of investigation (whatever that may be from one moment to the next)? Isn't it more a question of toggling between scales and angles, as one can frequently do in today's video games? When inside a character's head, we may want to switch to "Lacan mode." When following a swarm from above, "Deleuze mode" may be more appropriate. Or vice versa. Perhaps less played modes will yield more surprising and useful insights. In any case, *desire* here—and, indeed, *love*—is not a stable formula, lens, or diagram to be mapped onto unspooling phenomena according to a predetermined algorithm. Rather, it is a floating signifier, tethering and guiding subjects (or subject-effects) to the world in which they are thrown. As we will soon see, desire is not exclusively human. It is both an erogenous entry point to, and an exit wound from, our species-being.

3. See my book *Love and Other Technologies* (2006) for a more granular treatment of this specific theme.

4. In his book *A Lover's Discourse*, Barthes (1990, 190–91) writes that, "in the animal world, the release switch of the sexual mechanism is not a specific individual but only a form, a bright-coloured fetish (which is how the Image-repertoire starts up)." In making this connection, Barthes is essentially pointing to a continuum be-

tween the creaturely "sexual mechanism" and our own, somewhat more complex captivation by the beloved (perhaps by virtue of nothing more meaningful than the color of a piece of clothing or the line of cleavage or bicep), which we then reprocess through language into a self-sustaining narrative of intimate inevitability.

5. For Berlant (2012, 88), there are "three related kinds of popular culture that organize the conventional meanings of desire, gender, and sexuality: therapy culture, commodity culture, and liberal political culture."

6. Badiou (2012) has very many humanistic, even anthropocentric tendencies in his thinking. The human itself may be a kind of natural–historical "event" in his system. But almost despite himself, Badiou offers some moments where love might be considered not an achievement of the human, necessarily, but opening on to something more creaturely or worldly. "To love is to struggle," he writes, "beyond solitude, with everything in the world that can animate existence" (104).

## 1. Divining Creaturely Love

1. See Phillip Cary (2000), *Augustine's Invention of the Inner Self: The Legacy of a Christian Platonist,* in which the author explains how the proclamations following the Council of Nicea (A.D. 325) and the Council of Constantinople (A.D. 381) helped lead to an understanding of the human as, in effect, the first creature, of which Adam's animals are secondary artifacts of the divine Creator. Here was established the canonical notion of the Creator–creature distinction, "so essential to Christian theology, and so different from the pagan Neoplatonist scheme of emanation" (58).

2. Augustine's influence can still be detected in twentieth-century theology, such as in the discussion of creaturely love by the celebrated Russian Orthodox thinker Sergius Bulgakov (2002) in his magnum opus, *Bride of the Lamb*: "If divine love is unchanging and eternal, creaturely love is characterized by increase and decrease. It reflects the changing character of creaturely life" (156). And further in the same text: "God is love. He is love in Himself and in creation, which breathes by this power of love. In the spiritual world, this law of being is incomparably more transparent and more evident than in the human world. But creaturely love in creaturely limitedness, which is also creaturely freedom, also contains the possibility of unlove, which is the true source of satanism. Unlove, envy, hatred, all this is a cold flame, but one that is nonetheless lit from that one divine Love which is the sun of the world. But love is free, and God does not desire compulsion in love; He desires only persuasion. And He created free beings not as things but as self-determining personal centers. And the most profound self-determination to evil that has ever occurred in Satan, and extended to his angels" (507).

3. In his essay "The Divided Consciousness of Augustine on Eros," David Tracy (2005, 91) notes that this later pessimism came on the heels of an optimistic "*caritas* synthesis, in which Christian love as the pure gift of divine agape transforms but does not discard Platonic eros." For Augustine, *caritas* was the ideal, but the more he wrote, the more he saw evidence of its nemesis, *cupiditas*, love of the self alone (albeit through the image of the other).

4. See David Keck (1998, 106ff.) on the (sadly) lost science of "emotionology," which was partly engaged in speculatively examining the love lives of angels (especially across ranks). Interestingly, "good creatures" referred not only to humans in relation to God but to our own favorite commodities in relation to ourselves. Take, for instance, the reference to wine as "a good familiar creature" in Shakespeare's *Othello* or to "the good creature Tobacco" in early colonial histories. (See Thomas Hutchinson, *The History of the Colony of Massachusetts-Bay* [1765], as referenced by the *OED*.)

5. Even the pioneering American philosopher and semiotician Charles Sander Peirce had occasion to use the phrase in his 1893 essay titled "Evolutionary Love" (himself quoting Henry James's essay "Substance and Shadow"): "It is no doubt very tolerable finite or creaturely love to love one's own in another [*sic.*], to love another for his conformity to one's self: but nothing can be in more flagrant contrast with the creative Love, all whose tenderness *ex vi termini* [from the force of the term] must be reserved only for what intrinsically is most bitterly hostile and negative to itself" (1992, 353).

## 2. Horsing Around

1. The seeds of this section were first planted for a presentation, "A Horse Is Being Beaten: On Nietzsche's 'Equanimity,'" at the Tunnels, Tightropes, Mesh, and Networks symposium hosted by Theory Centre at Western University, visiting the New School (April 13, 2013). The proceedings are forthcoming from Punctum Press in a volume titled *Digital Dionysus: Nietzsche and the Network-centric Condition,* edited by Dan Mellamphy and Nandita Biswas Mellamphy.

2. I myself read Nietzsche's expression as closer to sardonically mischievous.

3. For a more detailed discussion of the ways in which totemic thinking and symbolism continue to inform the twenty-first-century mediascape, see my book *Look at the Bunny: Totem, Taboo, Technology* (2013).

4. Freud (1965, 68–69) writes, "The ego's relation to the id might be compared with that of a rider to his horse. The horse supplies the locomotive energy, while the rider has the privilege of deciding on the goal and of guiding the powerful animal's movement. But only too often there arises between the ego and the id the not precisely ideal situation of the rider being obliged to guide the horse along the path by which it itself wants to go." This is in itself a recasting of Plato's analogy in *The Phaedrus,* in which paired horses represent the body and the chariot rider the soul.

5. We might say, then, that if *Schadenfreude* is the perverse, neurotic pleasure one gets from seeing others fail or suffer, then *Schadennietzsche* is the healthy, noble glow one gets from seeing others triumph, rejoice, and overcome. It logically follows that someone who experiences the latter would also be more distressed at the scene of suffering than someone more inclined to the former.

6. In fourteenth-century Europe, a horse was the equivalent of a sports car, only much more so, since if a young peasant could secure one—by, say, ambushing a knight in the woods—then he was granted access into a world of prestige, privi-

lege, and relative power. Ownership of such an animal, no matter how obtained, allowed instant upward mobility—at least for a time. The great invention that enabled the rise of this new class of socioeconomic centaurs was the stirrup. Both McLuhan and Deleuze had much to say about this new technology, which created an unprecedented interspecies war machine. The horse–human–armor–lance assemblage became one lethal galloping event. "Few inventions have been so simple as the stirrup, but few have had so catalytic an influence on history," writes McLuhan (1997). "Antiquity imagined the Centaur; the early Middle Ages made him the master of Europe" (33). Moreover, it is arguable that the horse is the second cyborg, after humans, given that we find evidence of equine armor more than four thousand years ago in Persia. Medieval horses lugged as much metal as their riders did during battle. And of course, the horseshoe allowed horses to haul their loads far longer than previously possible, enhancing the animal for trade and industry. (As Desmond Morris [1989, 1] noted, perhaps courting controversy, "if a dog is man's best friend, the horse has been man's best slave.") Indeed, whenever we "harness" the power of Nature, we unconsciously figure the forces of *phusis* as equine in character.

7. As the centaurs themselves ask in Ovid's *Metamorphoses*, "what of our double strength? Has nature combined in ourselves the courage and force of the world's two mightiest creatures for nothing?" (488).

8. For Jacques Derrida (2009, 85–86), centaurs as a mythic class "represent the most asocial savagery . . . in particular because of their unbridled sexuality, which makes them attack women and wine." And yet, consistent with their chimerical composition, they can also be held up as a "model of ethics" (as Homer does of Chiron, once again, "the most just among centaurs" [86] and an excellent teacher besides).

9. Glenn Most (2005, 44) reminds us that, "in early Greek lyric poetry, the temporal immortality of the beloved or of the lover is celebrated in the image of a bird, which is unencumbered by spatial limitations." Of course, such neo-Hellenic allusions were commonplace among the educated classes of this time. Nietzsche's fondness would become embittered, however, as so often happens when the passions are aroused, as he considered challenging Rée to a duel and described Salomé in a letter as "a dried up, dirty, ill-smelling monkey with false breasts" (in Wolfenstein 2000, 192).

10. As Zarathustra would say to his animal entourage, a year or two after horsing around with Salomé, "You are my proper animals. I love you. But I still lack the proper human beings!" (in Silverman 2009, 58).

11. Anat Pick's (2011) seductive notion of "creaturely poetics" in fact abolishes any distinction between language and materiality, preferring instead to argue that the two are entangled in profound and inherent ways. She writes that the creature within creaturely poetics is not merely figural but "first and foremost a living body—material, temporal, and vulnerable" (5)—and that the blurring of boundaries between the human and the animal occurs in on the register of "intersomaticity" (15). Although I have great sympathy for Pick's extension or adaption of Santner's motif—which seeks to emphasize exposure and obligation, rather

than protection and rights, of the nonhuman (whether located in the other or the self)—my own version of the creaturely follows a different path than hers. Pick's creature is the protagonist of a possible "'rehabilitation' of religious discourse" and ancillary notions of framing (bare) life as postsecular or even saintly, thanks to her interest in the ethicoreligious project of Simone Weil, in particular. My understanding of the creature owes more to genealogies and trajectories of immanence, unfolding as far as (in)humanly possible from the whiff of the thurible.

12. As Breon Mitchell (1990) notes, when it comes to animals and the symbols they seem to bring with them, there is a symptomatic ambivalence lodged in the heart of such high humanists as Salomé. Whether other forms of life are considered in terms of ontological lack or surplus, a conceptual distance is created, and the exceptionalism of the human is reinforced: "The realm of creatures to be understood here, as elsewhere, as the nonhuman realm of universal creation, that which is *merely* creation. Or, expressed positively, that which is still *fully* creation, not simply a less human, auxiliary creation. That Lou Andreas-Salomé 'instinctively draws these comparisons from the realm of creatures' not only indicated the 'limited nature of all human measure' but also says something about her. It illustrates that, for her, the most forceful and direct language stems from the 'realm of creatures' and not of man. There is no infidelity in that realm. The phrase 'love of animals' means nothing—'love for creatures' says everything" (215). The same commentator goes on to note that "the equation of creature with the nonhuman realm of universal creation may be indebted to the phrasing of Romans 8, 19" (215). (From the King James Bible: "For the earnest expectation of the creature waiteth for the manifestation of the sons of God. For the creature was made subject to vanity, not willingly, but by reason of him who hath subjected the same in hope, Because the creature itself also shall be delivered from the bondage of corruption into the glorious liberty of the children of God. For we know that the whole creation groaneth and travaileth in pain together until now.")

13. The key critical reference here is Eric Santner's (2006) *Creaturely Life*, which discusses Rilke in biopolitical terms, along with Kafka and Sebald. This compelling and brilliant book tracks specific vectors and sites of power, exposure, *jouissance*, and infrahumanity in literature and modern(ist) life, informing my own work in many respects. For Santner, "creaturely life" essentially designates the type of vitality marked, incited, excited, and crippled by exposure to the capricious sovereignty of the Big Other. It takes a different path, however, in terms of the exceptionalism or location of the key category. Where Santner reserves the creaturely as an agonistic space only for the compromised human to *fall into*, as it were (since it is created by the law and the symbolic), I would prefer to consider it a place in which *all* creatures might find themselves, no matter how fleetingly, or how differently—for better or for worse. In other words, Santner's "creaturely life" is a form of life suffered (and perversely enjoyed) only by "artists formerly known as human." In contrast, I see "creaturely love" as a mode of existence that cannot be used to ontologically privilege ourselves, even in a negative light. My concept refuses to reinforce an assumed gulf between us and other beings, even as it seeks to

avoid collapsing all creatures into some kind of fantastic cosmopolitan multitude. Rather, it invites all manner of singular and situated entanglements and confusions, hopefully avoiding any (ultimately reassuring) pathos of a latent and abject humanism. (For more on this distinction, see "After the Beep: Answering Machines and Creaturely Life," in my book *Human Error: Species-Being and Media Machines* [2011].)

14. Rilke's sensitivity at times went beyond the animal kingdom to embrace plants, as in this remarkable moment of intense vegetal empathy, which appears in a 1914 letter to Salomé: "I am like a little anemone that I once saw in my garden in Rome. It had opened up so wide during the day that it could not close during the night! It was terrible to see it in the dark meadow, wide open, still inhaling everything through its wide-open throat—with the much too imposing night above that would not be consumed. And nearby, the clever sisters, each closed up around its small body. I too am incurably exposed and vulnerable. For this reason I am totally distractable; I decline nothing. My senses respond to the least disturbance without asking my permission" (Andreas-Salomé 2003, 80).

15. In her memoir of their relationship, Salomé (2003) notes that in 1920, Rilke's Swiss friends "gave him a fortuitous gift; they provided him with a castle, Schloss Bergam Irchel, in the canton of Zurich. [He wrote]: 'This little old castle Berg—mine, for me quite alone, like the wintry solitude. Berg, far from any access by train, is difficult to reach, more so because of the quarantine imposed on account of lockjaw and hoof-and-mouth disease, it is even more remote. Consequently, I have not been able to leave the boundaries of the park for weeks—but each limitation of this kind only reinforces my protection and safety'" (101). This little historical wrinkle is as revealing as it is trivial: a localized bovine virus functions serendipitously as a Muse for one of the most celebrated poetic sequences of the twentieth century. After all, they say a writer thrives on restrictions; and this particular writer—wrestling with angels on the ramparts of friends' castles for the soul trapped within finitude—thrived on creaturely inspired travel restrictions. No matter how angelic the flights of language take him, the Poet can still be infected!

## 3. Groping for an Opening

1. Jean-Christophe Bailly (2011) offers the elegant and economical definition of the Open as "nothing but an eternal presentation to the present" (18).

2. Giorgio Agamben's (2004) book *The Open* discusses the polarized readings of the Open by Rilke and Heidegger. The latter, with his emphasis on the exceptional potential of human *Dasein*, believed animals to be essentially trapped or captivated by this ontological case of antiagoraphobia, whereas "Man" has at least the prospect of using language and other forms of *technē* to fully accede to Being (beyond physiological imperatives and/or psychological foreclosures).

3. Salomé reinforces the point, image, and language in her reminisces: "It is the body that does not allow itself to be part of the desired unity, resists it and is hedged between the animal and the angel ([Rilke's letter dating] Paris, June 26, 1914): 'My body has become like a trap'" (2003, 94).

4. Lauren Berlant's (2011) recent book of this title so convincingly argues the prevalence and historical mutation of this inherent aspect of "love" that any discussion of affective experience and self-narration is limited without recourse to the seductive self-limitations of "cruel optimism."

5. Kaja Silverman's (2009) beautiful book *Flesh of My Flesh* discusses Salomé's and Rilke's correspondence in terms of the cosmic analogies which puncture and punctuate our creaturely lives and loves. My thinking is greatly indebted to her nuanced discussion of ontology, aesthetics, and (un)fated intimacies.

## 4. Electric Caresses

1. As one of my colleagues said to me recently, proudly displaying a photo of the new family dog, "It is true. I have a weakness for handsome men."

2. Karen Barad's (2015) piece, "On Touching," complicates our hopelessly anachronistic notions of the physics of touch in intriguing and challenging ways, taking into account quantum field theory and the material entanglements and affective intensities it invokes. Sadly, I am not qualified to follow very far down this highly specialized rabbit hole and so will linger with Euclidean cats and Newtonian legs.

## 5. Between Perfection and Temptation

1. Musil's most prominent public appearance was to deliver a very well received address in Berlin in 1927, in honor of the recently departed Rilke, to whom he had written a fan letter as a young man.

2. At least one commentator speculates that Musil's unorthodox upbringing, in which his mother's (male) lover lived in the same house as her husband and child for many years, was the source of much of the writer's fascination with ambiguous erotic geometries and elective affinities (Thiher 2009, 2).

3. It is presumably the lure of the wild beast, in contrast to the sluggish husband, that accounts for the current popularity of bigfoot and dinosaur erotica: a subgenre that has helped increase some self-published authors' bank accounts to the tune of thirty thousand dollars a month. (See the respective online articles by Crocker [2014] and O'Conner [2013].) Such trends dovetail neatly with at least one recent voice in the incessant public chatter about gender: Daniel Bergner's *What Do Women Want? Adventures in the Science of Female Desire*, which argues—as if for the first time!—that female sexuality is "base, animalistic and ravenous" (in Clark-Flory 2013).

4. Literary critic and Musil specialist Allen Thiher (2009, 89) notes, "To be excited by an animal odor bespeaks . . . [Claudine's] desire to attach herself to something raw and carnal that will deprive her of personal identity."

5. In one of the several significant references to marionettes throughout the lectures composing *The Beast and the Sovereign*, Derrida (2009, 251) states that they are "a technical thing, and even a sort of allegorical personification of technical power itself." As such, puppets and marionettes are parallel figures to the creature, in terms of revealing the latent (or potential) inhumanity of the human.

6. Silverman (2009, 173) insists that "an analogy is a very different thing from a meta-

phor. A metaphor entails the substitution of one thing for another. This is a profoundly undemocratic relationship, because the former is a temporary stand-in for the latter and because it only has provisional reality. In an analogy, on the other hand, both terms are on equal footing, ontologically and semiotically. They also belong to each other at the most profound level of their being."

7. Sadly, Silverman (2009, 40) lapses into post-Heideggerian humanism when she states, "What distinguishes us from other creatures is our capacity to *affirm* these correspondences." Yet in the same breath she admits that the key analogy of finitude "links us to every other living being" and is therefore "infinitely extendable" (41).

8. Class or social station is the silent factor in Musil's depictions of women, and it is the petty-bourgeois upbringing of both Claudine and Veronica that provokes the taboo attraction–repulsion to the animalistic, in the first case, and the animal proper, in the second. Peasant women, however, especially of the foreign variety, are far more laissez-faire with their thoughts and bodies, in Musil's view, though not without interiority. As we find in the short story "Grigia," they are reconciled with their nonhuman side: "The women lower their eyelids and keep their faces quite stiff, a defensive mask, so as not to be disturbed by one's curiosity. They let scarcely a moan escape them. Motionless as beetles feigning death, they concentrate all their attention on what is going *on* within them" (Musil 1999a, 33). In his discussion of the protagonist of this story, who resembles the author more than a little, Thiher (2009, 126) observes "a prime example of the species of European man who wants his Christian romanticism and his biological bestiality at the same time. . . . In short, [the male protagonist] is a pig looking for eternity." Not a bad description of the majority of twentieth-century literary characters of the masculine persuasion.

9. Another one of Veronica's erotic temptations is instructive here: "So they stood side by side. And as the wind came blowing more and more strongly along the road and was like some marvellously soft and fragrant animal laying itself upon things, on her face, on the nape of her neck, in her armpits . . . breathing everywhere, its soft velvety fur overlaying everything and, at every breath she drew, pressing tighter on her skin . . . both her horror and her expectation dissolved in a languid warmth that began to circle round her, mute and blind and slow, like blood blown by the wind. And suddenly she could not help thinking of something she had once been told: that millions of infinitesimal living entities have their habitation on every human being and that with every drawn breath and every breath exhaled there are incalculable rivers of life that come and go. She lingered for an instant in astonishment at this thought, feeling a warmth and a darkness as though being borne along in a huge crimson wave" (204). The animal is no longer confined to those molar entities of which we have known the names since Adam. Instead, it roams the landscape, in molecular ubiquity. If creaturely life is the embodied experience of a cringing and excited exposure to the unpleasable sovereign, then creaturely love—at least as Musil depicts it—is a similar affective complex, but without the key orientation point of the sovereign's avatars. Desire is shown to be

both more and less than human: always struggling to move beyond the narrow confines of so-called civilized copulation rituals. So to say, creaturely love is, in these stories, revealed to be ecological, and thus patched together from the materiality of things, things that cannot be introjected by the ego. It is neither centrifugal nor centripetal but something closer to the cycles of condensation that create drought or flood. Again, it is experienced as an atmosphere and as no less influential on the sequence of events than the climate.

## 6. The Biological Travesty

1. There is much to be said about the totemic power of fur in countless erotic encounters. The fur is a crackling second skin, a souvenir of the hunt, allowing Rilke's "electric caresses" to be transferred from the wild, or only partially domesticated, animal to the human. The fur is at once the height of sophistication and the material trace of musky bestiality. Hence the erotic charge of Leopold von Sacher-Masoch's *Venus in Furs* (1870)—a paradoxical figure that embodies both pagan divinity and modern sexual identity. (Hence Musil's fetishistic disquiet when in the presence of his mother's fur coat.) The fur is a sanctioned costume to dress oneself up as a chic creature, wavering between person and persona, predator and prey. It is a pelt that the man can carry away as trophy of his quarry or that the woman can use—as in Sacher-Masoch's tale—to reverse the gendered power structure, at least in the liminal and phantasmatic space of the bedroom. It is not surprising, then, that men, hearing the siren song of women's equality becoming louder and louder, began to redouble their efforts to domesticate their wives and put them on a leash. Fourier (2011)—who has been credited with inventing the word *feminism*, if not the idea—well understood the relation between antlers and fur, jealousy and desire, animality and animosity. After all, to whom does the cuckold proffer his eulogies of marriage? "Most often it is to the one who gives him his horns" (14).

2. A remarkable parallel with Rilke is the fact that Musil was also born after the death of a sister, complicating his relationship to mortality and gender: "her name was Elsa . . . my sister who died before I was born and who was the object of a kind of cult of mine. Evidently there are connections here! (In truth, I did not carry on any cult; but this sister interested me. I sometimes used to wonder what it would be like if she were still alive—would I be the person who was closest to her? Did I put myself in her place? There was no motive to do so. However, I do remember from the time when children wore a smock that I, too, sometimes wanted to be a girl.)" (Musil 1998, 468). Long sections of quasi-incest between Ulrich and Agathe in *The Man without Qualities* belies his denial that Elsa had a cultish fascination for him.

3. A woman's coat makes another cameo appearance in Musil's diaries, although only posthumously, via a reference in the preface by the editors. This concerns a passage where Musil considers Martha "objectively" during one of her rare jealous fits, playing a "game" with himself, wondering what it would be like to leave her or, rather, let her leave him. As Philip Payne notes in the preface, "the diary entry in question was recovered [in 1980] some years after Martha Musil's death, sewn into the lining of her coat—one wonders whether she wanted to suppress the evidence

of Musil's trifling with her feelings, or whether, by contrast, she treasured the lines as testimony of his actual fidelity" (Musil 1998, xxvii–xxviii).

4. Musil (1998, 412): "The kind of behavior that I once called, provisionally, 'ratioid' and 'non-ratioid' refers to the two underlying modes of conduct, which are given with human history—namely, the mode of the 'unequivocal' and that of 'analogy.' . . . The second basic principle is that of analogy. The logical remainder of the dream, of religious feeling, {vision}, (intuition), of the a Z. [*der andere Zustand*: the "other" condition], of morality, of creative writing."

5. In another case of literary animal totemism, a couple of decades later, "Christopher Isherwood and his young lover, Don Bachardy, assumed the playful roles of, respectively, Dobbin the Horse and Kitty the White Cat. . . . 'A cruel truth about the Animal personae,' Isherwood writes, 'is that they could be deployed falsely, thereby maintaining a sentimental fiction of harmony when there was none'" (in Greenberg 2014, 30).

6. Instead, Musil wrote an enigmatic short story, "The Blackbird" (Musil 2006), in which a blackbird brings his narrator strange crepuscular dreams, embodying at once his mother and his wife. Moreover, "another kind of character still exists side by side with the embodiment that human beings take on in their day-to-day existence, just as in fairy tale times the gods took on the forms of snakes and fish" (162).

7. Elsewhere, Musil makes another observation designed to give the humanist pause: "As to the psychology of sheep: The finely chiseled expression of exalted consciousness is not unlike the look of stupidity" (Musil 2006, 19).

8. This is not to promote the wholesale projection of human characteristics onto other creatures or to try to extend the sovereign circle of personhood to certain "higher" animals. Rather, it is to recognize the fact that certain characteristics that define our sense of selfhood emerge from prehuman and prepersonal places—in this instance, the shared pleasure–pain anticipation of being tickled.

## 7. "The Creature Whom We Love"

1. Nussbaum (2005) places Proust in the lineage of both Plato and Spinoza, who similarly seek to trace the archetypal line of this contemplative ascent, in which "the cure for the vulnerability of passion is the passion for understanding . . . [so that] one finds oneself able to deal with the very same worldly objects . . . without agonizing dependency, without ambivalence and the desire for revenge, without the self-centered partiality that makes love a threat in the social life" (227).

2. In the Montcrieff and Kilmartin translation, of which I am most familiar, "creature" is usually a translation of the French *créature*. However, it can also be used for *bête*, which itself has a profound and singular cluster of meanings for the French ("animal," "silly," etc.): something Derrida has discussed at length, especially in his lecture series, *The Beast and the Sovereign* (2009).

3. Even though the pun does not hold in the original French, "Swann in love" seems to acknowledge the unhuman aspect of intense passion and evoke Ovidian echoes of metamorphosis. The theory that this synchronicity is somewhat deliberate is

strengthened by the story of Proust's real-life use of the swan as a totem for his beloved chauffeur, Alfred Agostinelli, who is considered by many to be the male model of Albertine. See Carson (2014).

4. In the book, as in the culture of the time, male homosexuality is the bigger crime, partly because physical love between women was seen as somehow frivolous and inconsequential (even impossible). There is also the right civilized people reserve for themselves to make an exception in the case of those blessed with exceptional beauty, as when Robert de Saint-Loup asks the narrator, "What were we talking about? Oh yes, that big, fair girl, Mme. Putbus's maid. She goes with women too, but I don't suppose you mind that, I can tell you frankly, I have never seen such a gorgeous creature" (Proust 2006, 92).

5. There is, of course, a long and inglorious history of stigmatizing homosexuality as "creaturely" in the most pejorative, even criminal, sense. Even today, a Mexican politician, Ana Maria Jimenez Ortiz, felt confident enough to state in public that gay men should not be allowed to legally marry, because they don't face each other while having sex (the sure sign, apparently, of human intercourse). "Who pretends to love decently," she said, "using the favorite position of dogs?" (see Barber 2013). Thankfully the male gay global community has acquired a resilient sense of humor in the ongoing chorus of such insults, with many preferring to perform and enjoy their own creaturely attractions via the totemic figure of the bear.

6. See Rich's (2005) transcribed lecture from the University of Chicago, "Proust among the Animals."

## 8. The Love Tone

1. In his diary, Musil rationalizes his appreciation of the bodies of adolescent girls by inserting the qualification that "perversity only makes an appearance if a person feels a desire to abuse this dream of form in reality. Then he has to disregard the spirit and innocence (or helplessness) of the child, and also the absence of a sexual response; it is as if he wanted to go to bed with a doll or like a rutting frog, clasping a piece of wood" (454). A more Uexküllian view of the matter would be harder to find. (And here we might simply note in passing the captive and creaturely sign that Nabokov bestows on his nymphets, associated so explicitly with the butterfly net.)

2. See Uexküll's charming sketches of how he imagines that different animals "see" the world.

3. In some remarkable footage from a 1970s episode of the BBC's *World of Wonder*, a frog in a lab responds instantly to a horizontal strip of cardboard, which it mistakes for a caterpillar, by darting out its long tongue. But the same frog does not respond at all when the same piece of cardboard is flipped vertically. The latter shape is outside the frog's *Umwelt*—it has a different perception image—and is thus invisible to it, physiologically and ontologically. Which begs the question, to how many equivalents of this vertical strip of cardboard are humans completely oblivious?

4. Uexküll sounds less like a scientist, however, when he describes the collective *Um-*

*welten* as fitting together in a cosmic and harmonic musical score: one, moreover, not free of "meaning." According to Uexküll's vision, in Nature, "nothing is left to chance, but rather, that the animal and its medium are everywhere connected by an intimate meaning rule which binds the two in a duet in which the properties of both partners are composed contrapuntally to one another? Only extreme deniers of meaning as a natural factor will want to deny that, in the functional cycle of gender, males and females are composed for each other according to meaning, and assert that the love duet which permeates the entire living world in a thousand variations arose without a plan. In the love duet of animals and human beings, two partners of equal status face each other, each of which rules as a subject and appears as a recipient of meaning in his environment, while the role of carrier of meaning is given to the other partner. The perception organs as well as the effect organs are contrapuntally arranged toward one another in both partners" (2000, 174–75). Nowhere here is the agony, ecstasy—or even androgyny—of Proustian passion.

5. Which is not simply to merge human and nonhuman biosemiotics into a single homogenous mass. See Cary Wolfe's important comments regarding "the technicity of a semiosis that is radically *not ours* and radically *not us*" (in Broglio 2013, 185).

6. To take merely one example, see Bagemihl (2000).

7. To quote Derrida (2008) in more detail: "The narcissistic identification of one's fellow of the same species also works through the play of call and response between voices, of singing and sonic productions that are both coded and inventive. Wherever reproduction functions by means of sexual coupling (and that marks one of the important frontiers, subfrontiers, between so many animals or different species), well then, one has to register some mirror effect—visual, aural, indeed olfactory—some hetero-narcissistic 'self as other.' Especially when—and this is where one sees the intertwining of threads that until now seemed to be entangled without order or without law—this hetero-narcissism is erotic: once the specularity of one's fellow is understood to begin with sexual difference, on the eve of, but already involved in the technical stage of mirroring, of narcissistic or echographical mirroring, account has to be taken of the seductive pursuit without which there is no sexual experience, and no desire or choice of partner in general" (60).

## 9. "The Soft Word That Comes Deceiving"

1. We could well consider Master Richard to be an ancestor of the male voice in John Donne's early-seventeenth-century poem "The Flea," given the insistent imagination with which both men marshal animal figures to mediate and advocate their cause: "Mark but this flea, and mark in this / How little that which thou deniest me is; / It sucked me first, and now sucks thee, / And in this flea our two bloods mingled be; / Thou know'st that this cannot be said / A sin, nor shame, nor loss of maidenhead."

2. The motif of the hunt becomes more gruesome still in the hands of the Marquis de Sade, who of course goes beyond seduction for sport to the pure sadism

associated with his name and writings. The term *creature* is one of Sade's literary tics, deployed frequently to estrange the human context of the victims, while emphasizing the distance between culture and Nature (for what perverse pleasure is there to be taken in reducing a being to an animal, if it is *already* an animal?). In his mercifully brief book *Philosophy in the Bedroom,* Sade (1990) introduces us to Madame de Saint-Ange, a libertine who nevertheless seeks to enhance her dark *jouissance* by combining all of God's creatures into one. "I am an amphibious creature," she confesses to her brother. "I love everything, everyone, whatever it is, it amuses me; I should like to combine every species" (187).

## 10. The Cuckold and the Cockatrice

1. According to Grose (1796), "to have the horn" describes "a temporary priapism."
2. In French slang, *cerf* (stag) denotes a cuckold. Rowland implies that the association of horns with the cuckold can be traced back to the story of Acteaon, which she reads as an allegory for the trauma of discovered adultery. For a close reading of Tolstoy's devastating tale of this theme, see my chapter "Tolstoy's Bestiary: Animality and Animosity in *The Kreutzer Sonata*" in Pettman (2013).
3. A later, and more overdetermined, attempt to systematize romantic behavior for the benefit of society at large was Aron Zalkind's "Twelve Commandments for the Sexual Revolution of the Proletariat," published in Soviet Russia in 1925. Number 9 of this libidinal–economic manifesto reads, "Sexual partners should be selected on the basis of class." ("Sexual attraction to class antagonism, to a morally disgusting, dishonest object, is as perverse as the sexual desire of a human for a crocodile or an orangutan.") Quoted in Proctor (2013).
4. Ethologists talk with a straight face of the "sneaky fucker" strategy, whereby beta males take advantage of the distraction created by aggressive alpha males to have their way with the females under dispute (Cherfas 1977, 673). Indeed, scientific studies continue to have the virtue of considering human courting rituals and tactics through lenses borrowed from evolutionary biology. To take only one of countless examples, consider Tracy Vaillancourt's (2013) psychological study, which asks in its title, "Do human females use indirect aggression as an intrasexual competition strategy?" Specifically on the question of fidelity in the animal kingdom, see Barash and Lipton (2001). In an interview with the *New York Times* (Angier 2008), the authors can point to only one single species "in which there seems to be 100 percent monogamy," that being *Diplozoon paradoxum*—a flatworm that lives in gills of freshwater fish. But how can they be so sure? "Males and females meet each other as adolescents, and their bodies literally fuse together, whereupon they remain faithful until death."

## 11. The Animal Bride and Horny Toads

1. Sax notes that there are also "animal groom" stories, popularized in the West in tales such as Madame de Beaumont's "Beauty and the Beast," the Grimm Brothers' "The Frog King," and George Dasent's "East of the Sun and West of the Moon" (78). These are less common, however.

2. Sax also reads the Cinderella story as a humanized version of the animal bride legend, where glass slippers replace the skin of a seal, or some other trace of her creaturely origin, when the woman suddenly quits the scene (69). He also discusses Hans Christian Andersen's *The Little Mermaid* in some detail. In this story, the protagonist "goes to a sea witch for help. The hag gives the mermaid a potion that will change her fish tail into legs, adding that every step the mermaid takes will bring pain" (154). It is tempting to read this transformation as an allegory about the invention of high-heeled shoes and the sacrifice women were just starting to make to be more socially and spatially mobile. (Andersen's father was a shoemaker, after all!)

3. For a notable twentieth-century take on the animal bride story, see Garnett's (1985) novella *Lady into Fox* (written 1922), whose title economically distills the conceit of the tale. The wife's transformation is as sudden as it is unexplained, leaving the perplexed husband to care for his equally astonished creaturely companion, as she becomes more and more foxlike (until any latent human characteristics all but vanish). Like Ovid, animal bride stories, and folktales, Garnett literalizes the creaturely metaphors we use to describe love, even as he also provides a modern allegory for one woman's somatic resistance to domesticity.

4. The source here is identified in the original simply as a "Carrier Indian."

5. In his recent book, Kohn (2013) dismantles the rigid distinction between humans and animals based on the symbolic realm, arguing that nonhuman living beings (both fauna and flora) constantly engage in their own forms of "representation" or nonsymbolic semiosis. He calls this highly intersubjective process "the living thought" (see esp. chapter 2).

6. At the end of *The Open*, Agamben (2004) seems to suggest that a form of creaturely love, or at least animal-headed sex, affords a way to crash the operating system of the anthropological machine and thus gain access to inoperable inhumanity. Writing several years earlier, Sax (1998) also looks forward to a similar millennial reconciliation with our animal origins: "If human beings ever overcome their alienation, the very definition of 'humanity' will change. Though perhaps almost unaltered biologically, in a sense people will have become extinct. We will have blended with the myriad forms of life, out of which, long ago, we emerged. The moral distinction between a man and an elephant may mean no more than that between a sparrow and a swan" (220).

7. Another French proverb underlines the unhuman aspect of intercourse: "si une fois une fille a fait l'amour, j'amerais mieux garder un pré rempli de belettes" (once a girl has made love, I would rather look after a meadow full of weasels) (in Rowland 1973, 159).

8. Rowland (1973, 92) writes, "A bas-relief underneath a console on the façade of the cathedral church of Saint-Jeans at Lyons dating from the fifteenth century depicts the philosopher in his humiliating position. Behind him lurks the hare, the symbol of libidinousness." It is perhaps also worth mentioning here that the term *whore* comes from the Middle English word for "hare," just as the rabbit *(cuniculus)* has been traditionally associated with the vagina *(cunnus)*. Were a medieval

Englishman transported to contemporary Brooklyn, he would likely assume Coney Island to be anything but a family-friendly destination.

9. Rowland (1973, 105) observes that "in every language riding is a commonplace term for coitus. In Germany a feeble lover is called a *Sonntagsreiter* (a Sunday rider) . . . and the honeymoon can be termed *Stutenwocke* (mare week)."

10. The history of the *charivari*—a public intervention and form of folk justice (of which the "scold's bridle" is a vicious example)—is a troubling one for us modern liberal subjects, who would place the rights and privacy of the individual above the "pack" of the agitated public addressing a "wrong" such as a "shrewish" woman or a childless marriage.

## 12. Unsettled Being

1. The eponymous protagonist of J. M. Coetzee's (2003) novel *Elizabeth Costello* can't help but be curious about this kind of sexual intercourse between gods and mortals. "What intrigues her is less the metaphysics than the mechanics, the practicalities of congress across a gap in being. Bad enough to have a full-grown male swan jabbing webbed feet into your backside while he has his way, or a one-ton bull leaning his moaning weight on you; how, when the god does not care to change shape but remains his awesome self, does the human body accommodate itself to the blast of his desire?" (184). In Costello's opinion, the gods may be "awesome," but they also envy us our finitude, which provides a *frisson* they, in their Olympian ennui, cannot resist. "It is we who live the more urgently, feel the more intensely. . . . That, finally, is why they do not declare a ban on sex with us, merely make up rules about where and in what form and how often. Inventors of death; inventors of sex tourism too" (189).

2. Agamben (2014) notes, "The Greek word for animal, *zoon*, means, literally, 'living being.' And for a Greek, a god was a 'living being' (even if the god's *zoe* is *ariste kai aidos*, 'optimal and eternal'). In their 'animal' nature—which is to say, their *living* nature—man and god commune. This is the reason gods take on animal form when they desire sexual union with humans." In Agamben's view, the Hellenic mystery cults were designed to reinforce the continuity between animal and deity, via the hinge of the human. "The living being lost in the animal rediscovered himself in the divine as he who was lost in the divine rediscovered himself in the animal." Christ would be the one to break this pagan trinity into three fractured spheres, "thereby condemning us to humanity" (43–45).

3. Or as Haraway (2008) might (not) say, "when species fail to meet."

4. Of course I am using this traditional sexual dynamic not as a historical constant but, again, as structuralist fable that informs all manner of gendered exceptions or experiments within and around the same power structure.

5. In Ovid's libidinal economy, divine forces can punish mortals for simply desiring too much; as happens with "girls who have been / inspired to a frenzy / of lawless passion and paid the price for their lustful desires" (389).

6. Ovid seems to sense the erotic ambiguities that not only encourage creaturely forms of intimacy but spark all manner of sudden mutations. In one tale, a flam-

boyantly dressed stag is a figure of fascination: "The boy Cyparíssus adored a stag / which was sacred to all the nymphs who haunt the Carthaéan plains, / a magnificent creature with spreading antlers that cast a shadow / above its head. The horns were brilliantly tipped in gold; / and over the shoulder, around the smooth round neck, they had hung / a collar studded with jewels. On its forehead there dangled a silver / amulet held by the lightest of thongs; while—no less fetchingly— / pendants of pearls gleamed down from its two ears next to the temples" (387).

7. It is certainly an amusing piece of historical continuity to think that ancient lovers could be caught cheating if they did not erase their tablets properly. As Ovid (2002) warns in *The Art of Love*, "And whenever you write one [a girlfriend] a letter, / You had better / Check the tablets for traces of a previous note: / Many a woman reads what her lover never wrote / To her" (84–85).

## 13. Fickle Metaphysics

1. In one fascinating aside, Ovid's Pythagoras notes, "Not long ago, in the temple of Juno at Argos, I noticed / a shield and knew that I once had borne it myself on my left arm! / All is subject to change and nothing to death" (602).

2. On this exhortation, Ovid's Pythagoras states, "I implore you, and mark my words. When you cram your mouths with the members / of slaughtered oxen, remember you're eating your own farm workers!" (600–601). And soon after: "What an impious shedding of human / blood is contrived, when the throat of a calf is slit with a knife, / and the ears of the butcher are deaf to its mother's pitiful lowing!" (616).

3. This continuity can be summed up in the case of the nymph Callisto: "But though her body was now a bear's, her emotions were / human" (71). And yet the text does appear to allow for the possibility of complete metamorphoses or an amnesiacal soul: "Now it appears that my human form is creeping away from me" (80).

4. Eiseley (1973, 6) renders Ovid's poetic flux scientifically sound when he also notes that "we are all potential fossils still carrying within our bodies the crudities of former existences, the marks of a world in which living creatures flow with little more consistency than clouds from age to age."

5. As Walter Benjamin writes (in Agamben 2011d, 6), "it is not that what is past casts its light on what is present, or what is present its light on what is past; rather, image is that wherein what has been comes together in a flash with the now *(Jetzt)* to form a constellation. In other words, image is dialectics at a standstill."

6. On this theme, Eiseley (1979, 216) quotes Emerson: "The transmigration of souls is no fable. I would it were; but men and women are only half human. Every animal in the barnyard, the field and the forest, of the earth and of the waters . . . has contrived to get a footing and to leave the print of its features and form in someone or other of these upright heaven-facing speakers."

7. Speaking of rhetorical or literary figures in general, Haraway (2008, 4) also refuses to cut the Gordian knot with Occam's razor, because "figures are at the same time creatures of imagined possibility and creatures of fierce and ordinary reality; the dimensions tangle and require response."

8. For Simondon (in Combes 2012, 6–7), beings "do not possess a unitary identity in a stable state in which no transformation is possible; beings possess transductive unity." I thank Erik Bordeleau (2013) for underscoring this phrase in his remarkable article "Soulful Sedentarity."

9. For a virtuoso discussion of this Aristotelian legacy, as debated by the twelfth-century Scholastics, as well as the implications for our own time, see Thacker (2010).

10. See Morton (2012).

11. As Thacker (2009, 32–33) has insisted, "the passport to the Other is always through others. The generic is metaphysical muzak for us. Logically, perhaps it can only be this. Morally, it soothes our apprehensions about that most Freudian guilt-trips—narcissism—at the species level. Do we—can we—ever love the generic in itself? Our language betrays its solipsism in the face of the generic. But I suppose that's what love is."

12. Eiseley (1979, 151) asks, "What if I am, in some way, only a sophisticated fire that has acquired an ability to regulate its rate of combustion and to hoard its fuel in order to see and walk?"

13. See Harman's (2002) book of the same name: arguably patient zero for the new field of object-oriented ontology.

## 14. Nymphomania and Faunication

1. One of the most recent "diagnoses" of a nymphomaniac is by Lars von Trier's film of the same name, regarding his protagonist with the androgynous name of "Joe." Trier's cinematic tale is framed both in the tradition of woman's dangerous, un-Christian sensual insatiability and in the spirit of subverting such a loaded pathologizing of female desire. (Nonhuman creatures figure in the film in the mode of implied analogy, such as the numerous fishing flies on the wall of the house in part 1—a visualization of the trappings of seduction and capture.)

2. Agamben here is talking specifically of Titian's *The Nymph and the Shepherd* (c. 1570–75), which is not to be confused with the Rupert Bunny painting reproduced in the main text, which, for me at least, captures the affect discussed more evocatively (perhaps by virtue of its more kitsch disposition).

3. Agamben's well-documented objection to DNA testing, checkpoint fingerprinting, and other biometrical operations stems from this unprecedented technical emphasis on the biological stratum of subjectivity: "identity without the person." He asks, "How is it possible to communicate with neither a smile nor a gesture, with neither graciousness nor reticence, but rather through a biological identity?" (2011a, 53–54). The irony here—one he doesn't seem interested in—is that the more "culture" evolves, the more biological we are rendered, the more we may recognize our kinship with our forever disavowed, and fellow, nonhuman creatures. The problem here, of course, is that no matter how many times we point toward "a danger which saves," the dangers multiply around us, very few of which have "our" interests at heart.

4. In Plato's *Symposium*, Socrates himself is described by the spurned Alcibiades as

a man who "clothes himself in language that is like the skin of the wanton satyr." Which makes one wonder why he is so afraid of being glamoured by nymphs, while sitting next to a stream, in the *Phaedrus*.

5. For a detailed and characteristically brilliant reading of the "the problem of nudity"—which is also "the problem of human nature in its relationship with grace"—see Agamben's (2011c) essay simply titled "Nudity."

6. Fournival (2000, 7) makes an interesting equivalence between clothing and love itself when he writes, "For as the monkey remains free as long as its feet are bare, and is not caught until it puts on shoes, so man is not imprisoned until he is in love."

7. After identifying something he calls "*the passion of the animal*" (11–12), Derrida (2008) links the seduction of/by nonhuman creatures with exhibitionism, simulation, and dissimulation, which then allows him to posit "a sort of rhetoric of modesty" (60) in animals. "But modesty or shame," he continues, "is, naturally . . . an aporetic movement, so self-contradictory, so exhibitionist within its very logic, that the most modest will always also be—this is the law of the symptom—the least modest. In the same movement the same ones will call woman the most modest and the most indecent. And, for the discourse that never resists placing the woman and child on the side of the animal, this is also the law that governs the nudity between what is called human and what I am calling the *animot*: the *animot* is more naked than the human, who is more naked than the *animot*" (57).

8. John Berger may be surprised that Derrida puts so much emphasis on the gaze of a pet, or what the former refers to as an "urban puppet." For Berger (1991, 28), "that look between animal and man, which may have played a crucial role in the development of human society, and with which, in any case, all men had always lived until less than a century ago, has been extinguished." Whether we agree with Berger probably depends on whether we class the pet as an animal, properly speaking, or whether this is a quasi-type of historically novel being.

## 15. Senseless Arabesques

1. The entire film hangs on Michelle Williams's restrained performance, which is at times reminiscent of a more humble and mundane Falconetti from *The Passion of Joan of Arc* (1928). In reviews, *Wendy and Lucy* was more often compared to the heart-wrenching neorealist classic *Umberto D.* (1952), given the depiction of love between a poverty-stricken person and their dog. Structurally speaking, it was also reminiscent of Polanski's *Frantic* (1988), in which the main character (Harrison Ford) searches, well, *frantically* for his missing wife through the streets of Paris. Reichardt's film, however, is on the polar opposite end of the continuum linking melodrama with its opposite.

2. For an illuminating reading of *Wendy and Lucy* through the lens of fatigue and endurance, see Gorfinkel (2012).

3. On a far less disturbing register—one of sadness rather than rage—the singer–songwriter Fiona Apple made headlines recently by publicly expressing her grief at the impending death of her pit bull Janet. In a letter posted online, Apple explains

that she is canceling her upcoming tour to be at her dog's side when she slips away: "She slept in bed with me, her head on the pillow, and she accepted my hysterical, tearful face into her chest, with her paws around me, every time I was heartbroken, or spirit-broken, or just lost, and as years went by, she let me take the role of her child, as I fell asleep, with her chin resting above my head. . . . She's my best friend and my mother and my daughter, my benefactor, and she's the one who taught me what love is. . . . I will not be the woman who puts her career ahead of love and friendship. I am the woman who stays home and bakes Tilapia for my dearest, oldest friend" (Battan 2012).

4. To pass the Bechdel test—named after the American feminist cartoonist Alison Bechdel—a work of fiction must feature at least two women talking to each other about something other than a man. It is remarkable how few Hollywood films pass such a test.

5. At the end of Ang Lee's film adaption of Yann Martel's *The Life of Pi* (2012), the protagonist, Pi Patel, is distraught when his tiger companion, "Richard Parker," simply lopes away into the trees once their lifeboat finds land. After their interspecies survival adventure, Pi believes they have reached an understanding—perhaps even a form of affection. But the tiger disappears without so much as a backward glance. This scene is designed to remind both the protagonist and the spectator that human–animal relationships are not at all conducted on the same terms or according to the same unwritten contract. What it fails to do, however, is acknowledge that people too often leave their lovers without such a sentimental glance, reminding us yet again that the stakes are between being and being, not reified human and symbolic animal.

## 16. The Goat in the Machine

1. See especially Pettman (2006).

2. Norway's recent "slow TV" project—which fixed a webcam on a tiny, hip café for birds—even acknowledges this aspect in the punning name *Piip Show* (i.e., "Peep Show").

3. In their recent coauthored and self-published book on commercial and media ecologies of cuteness, Law and Wark (2013) call such "kawaii" creatures "weaponized adorables."

4. See Gellman (2014).

5. As I write, the hugely popular dating site OKCupid is fighting a minor PR battle after admitting that it has been experimenting with people's profiles—going so far as to remove photos and change words—in the hope of yielding useful data about contemporary dating rituals (and presumably monetizing the same). One wishes they would subsequently change the name of their company to OKCupiditas.

6. I discuss *Her* in more detail in my forthcoming *Sonic Intimacy: Voice, Species, Technics*.

7. In a lovely observation, via his Twitter account, science writer James Gleik writes, "I'd say *Her* is a movie about (the education of) an interesting woman who falls in love with a man who, though sweet, is mired in biology."

8. Given the technical heritage of the very word and concept, we might even consider the "creature" as a form of "natural technics."

9. For more information, see the manufacturer's website: http://www.parorobots .com/.

10. Published on the *New York Times* website on June 17, 2015.

11. For a longer discussion of the love of objects, see Pettman and Clemens (2014). For a more sustained discussion of the contemporary love for "virtual girlfriends," see my piece "Love in the Time of Tamagotchi" in Pettman (2013). And for a provocative exploration of the possibility that machines may soon be more capable of exquisite erotic encounters than ourselves, see the hauntingly beautiful music video for Björk's "All Is Full of Love" as well as Shaviro's (2002) reading of this text.

12. It may be worth mentioning that (some) animals are willing to encounter (some) machines "on their own terms," as it were: as witnessed in the photographs and footage of hawks, goats, kangaroos, and other critters attacking drones, as if the latter were a natural predator or familiar prey.

13. For more on the notion of Pan, Dionysus, and "the goat in the machine," see Pettman (2002).

14. The French philosopher Anne Dufourmantelle (2007) reminds us that Deleuze's "desiring machine" is inspired in part by Spinoza, for whom "there are no desiring subjects, only subjects as modes or avatars of desire, that is, of thought." Dufourmantelle herself, deliberately playing cupid for a blind date between sex and philosophy, believes that the former "is there to remind us we are inhuman" (30). And though sex is said to be a bestial procedure, the question must be asked: "Are we so afraid of animals? Of what brings us closer to them?" (64).

## Conclusion

1. Indeed, Melville's tale often lapses into anthropomorphism, as when a diegetic scientific treatise on whales observes of the Right-Whale Porpoise: "In shape, he differs in some degree from the Huzza Porpoise, being of a less rotund and jolly girth; indeed, he is of quite a neat and gentleman-like figure. He has no fins on his back (most other porpoises have), he has a lovely tail, and sentimental Indian eyes of a hazel hue. But his mealy-mouth spoils all" (137). The phrase "Indian eyes" here reminds us that the perceptions and representations of race are a key aspect of creaturely discourse. For a very interesting recent study on the vexed nexus between race, sexuality, and animality, see Peterson (2013).

2. Dufourmantelle (2007, xvii) helpfully reminds us always to speak in plurals, because "even a locution such as '*the* body' reveals a mostly Western bias, since ayurveda, for instance, tallies up ten bodies and counting."

3. Silverman's conceptual accomplice, Leo Bersani, has recently introduced his notion of "repeatable being," which in many ways complements her expanded understanding of analogy. For Bersani, repeatable being "continuously fails to be unique—[and] creates a hospitable world of correspondences, one in which relations, no longer blocked by difference, multiply as networks of similitudes" (Bersani and Dutoit 2008, 117).

4. For David Halperin (2005, 55), love's final irony is the fact that "love imparts to creatures who are going to die an intuition of eternal reality." And yet there may indeed be a certain truth residing in this irony or paradox. So to say, finitude or mortality is not necessarily the end of the love story, since "passionate desire for an individual object always points somewhere beyond it, that no object contains within itself the secret of its own fascination" (54). Moreover, as Whitehead writes (in Eiseley 1979, 251), "we are . . . of infinite importance, because as we perish we are immortal."

5. Interestingly, Lucretius begins his great Epicurean poem-treatise *On the Nature of Things* with an elegy to love, as the force which animates all animated things: "enchained by delight" and following each other in "hot desire." See Porter (2005) for an illuminating discussion of this non-Christian genesis story and its influence on the father of psychoanalysis.

6. In his book *Sexual Behavior in the Human Female*, Alfred Kinsey (1998, 638) writes, "*Post coitum omne animal triste est, sive gallus et mulier*—After sex all animals are sad except the cock and the woman. This famous Latin proverb is originally attributed to Galen, a Greek physician from the 2nd century AD who linked the four temperaments sanguine, phlegmatic, choleric and melancholic to bodily dispositions. Sometimes (without the cock/woman add-on) Aristoteles is named as the author. But maybe it is just a universal truth of collective wisdom which can't be traced back to one single person."

7. Derrida points out that the still-hegemonic discourse of humanism relies on this distinction between "symbolic" thought and communication and the kind all other forms of life employ. The exceptionalism of the symbolic is also the key to Santner's (2006) concept of "creaturely life," which renders the human subject as something more abject, liminal, excited, and exposed than other beings: a quivering animal before the all-powerful gaze of the Other. In creaturely *love*, however, the beloved is a fusion of both Beast and Sovereign. So to say, when in love, we are exposed to the enigmatic appetites of the former and the capricious laws and states of exception of the latter.

8. Of course this is not to deny the historical and political importance of the Spectacle, as defined by critical theorists of the twentieth century, but to see what *other* things we might see—things we have missed for too long—if we temporarily bracket the Spectacle off, or look *through* it, with ultraviolet light.

9. See Thacker's (2013) gesture toward "a sort of *affective animal kingdom*" in Lautréamont, Bachelard, and others.

10. See Barthes's (2012) posthumously published lecture series, *How to Live Together,* for more on this extremely rich term and concept.

11. When viewing the human in the age of the intensified Spectacle, we are always employing a double exposure, even when using the naked eye. We see the human *and* the animal, which, after all, are at once coincident and fractured. This is why we cannot look at a picture of Audrey Hepburn without also seeing a cat, consciously or not.

George Cukor understood the comic potential of this double exposure when he spliced animal totems in tandem with the women they represent for the credits of *The Women* (1939)—lamb, fox, wild cat, owl, cow, and so on. In a much more tragic key, consider the use of the squirrel totem for Veronika, the female protagonist of the exquisite Soviet melodrama *The Cranes Are Flying* (1957).

12. The *pharmakon* is an ancient Greek concept, used by Plato and others, to denote something that can be both remedy and poison, depending on the context. More recently, this has been picked up as a descriptor for technology by Bernard Stiegler, via Derrida. See, for instance, Stiegler (2012).

13. For Eduardo Kohn (2013, 74–75), "life . . . is a sign process . . . albeit one that is often highly embodied and nonsymbolic."

14. In one of his *Pataphysical Essays* titled "On Human Fauna," the heterodox surrealist writer René Daumal (2012) introduces the whimsical art of "patagraphy." As distinct from photography, patagraphy is a "decomposing [of] the totality of a man." Such a process "reveals the animals of which he is the synthesis." Daumal goes on to explain: "The model of the man thus analyzed is the Sphinx, conforming to the image propounded by Socrates, who conceived of the human soul as a harmonious mix of sage, lion, and snake, all enclosed in the same bag of skin. Depending on the subject, and even depending on the moment, sometimes one animal will predominate over the other. . . . It will be noticed, then, that among those beings that we charitably call our fellow creatures, few deserve the designation of 'man' that we grant them. Nearly all of them are disguised animals. In truth, each man is the synthesis of a multitude of animals; but one of these animals has often developed to the detriment of the others, and although we believe we are addressing a man, it is rather a worm, a pike, a sheep, a wolf to which we are feeding the language that fattens him. Thanks to the intelligent practice of our patagraphic art, we will from now on be aware of with whom we are dealing" (39). The technology involved remains deliberately and amusingly ambiguous: a combination of industrial laboratory science and esoteric alchemy. A few pages later in the same essay, in a section called "Preparation of Patascopic Liquors," Daumal writes, "Let us suppose that we want a liquor capable of detecting goats. We place a well-chosen specimen of the animal in a field of our device. Our preference will be to use the mirror of solidified hydrogen. The focal sphere is filled with virgin pataplasm. We shall obtain the goat patagram. But we will have taken the precaution of making the beast fast for a week; we will have enforced an absolute sexual abstinence on his part for three months; deprived him of all movement for five days, of sleep for three days, and of drink for two days; we will have kept him for two weeks in a darkened room. The patagram thus produced will be an absolutely pure expression of the goat's desires" (41). This can then be used to trap the goat that lurks within most men.

15. For Bersani, we humans are psychically "darkened by the demand for love." Indeed, "to lose our fascinating and crippling expressiveness might be the precondition for our moving within nature, moving as appearances registering, and responding to

the call of, other appearances" (Bersani and Dutoit 2008, 70). No question this is a bracing and inspiring possibility. But one wonders how we might begin divesting ourselves of our "expressiveness," which is, after all, the quintessence of our solitary ontologies. Bersani would have us look for cues in the aesthetic realm, provided we understand such a realm as unburdened by "biographical density" (135) or "the seriousness of stable identities" (9). This new and radically open subjectivity or orientation would afford "exchanges with the world (exchanges which would be neither projections nor appropriations nor adaptive techniques)" (116).

16. Haraway (2008) prefers the more inclusive, and less theologically compromised, term *critter*: "I use the term critter to mean a motley crowd of lively beings including microbes, fungi, humans, plants, animals, cyborgs, and aliens" (330). In a sense, her entire body of work is a critical meditation on the parameters and possibilities of "critterly love."

17. The key term here is *transindividuation,* most closely associated with the work of Gilbert Simondon, unpacked in great detail more recently by Bernard Stiegler. For excellent commentary on the former, see Combes (2012), and for a representative reading of the latter, see Stiegler (2010).

18. In her famous "Cyborg Manifesto," Haraway (1991, 152) insists that "bestiality has a new status in this cycle of marriage exchange." See also my chapter "Zoocide: Animal Love and Human Justice" in *Human Error* (Pettman 2011).

19. To focus on the eye in such a way is to beg the question of whether I am attributing a *soul* to animals. A simple yes will suffice, if we recall Aristotle's definition of *psukhē* or "soul": the enigmatic animating principle of all living beings.

20. The poetic anthropologist Alphonso Lingis (2003, 171) essentially argues that *all* sex is bestiality: "when we make love with someone of our own species, we also make love with the horse and the calf, the kitten and the cockatoo, the powdery moths and the lustful crickets."

# BIBLIOGRAPHY

Agamben, Giorgio. 2004. *The Open: Man and Animal.* Palo Alto, Calif.: Stanford University Press.

———. 2011a. "Identity without the Person." In *Nudities.* Palo Alto, Calif.: Stanford University Press.

———. 2011b. "On What We Can Not Do." In *Nudities.* Palo Alto, Calif.: Stanford University Press.

———. 2011c. "Nudity." In *Nudities.* Palo Alto, Calif.: Stanford University Press.

———. 2011d. "Nymphs." In *Releasing the Image: From Literature to New Media,* ed. Jacques Khalip and Robert Mitchell. Palo Alto, Calif.: Stanford University Press.

———. 2014. *The Unspeakable Girl: The Myth and Mystery of Kore.* London: Seagull Books.

Andreas-Salomé, Lou. 1990. *Looking Back: Memoirs.* New York: Paragon House.

———. 2003. *You Alone Are Real to Me: Remembering Rainer Maria Rilke.* Rochester, N.Y.: BOA Editions.

Angier, Natalie. 2008. "In Most Species, Faithfulness Is a Fantasy." *New York Times,* March 18.

Archibald, Sasha. 2014. "Women Cuddling Animals." *New Inquiry,* January 3.

Augustine, St. 1982. *The Literal Meaning of Genesis.* Vol. 1. Mahwah, N.J.: Paulist Press.

———. 2012. *City of God: A Critical Guide.* Edited by James Wetzel. Cambridge: Cambridge University Press.

Badiou, Alain, with Nicolas Truong. 2012. *In Praise of Love.* London: Serpent's Tail.

Bagemihl, Bruce. 2000. *Biological Exuberance: Animal Homosexuality and Natural Diversity.* New York: Stonewall Inn Editions.

Bailly, Jean-Christophe. 2011. *The Animal Side.* New York: Fordham University Press.

Balthus. 1984. *Mitsou: Forty Images.* With an introduction by R. M. Rilke. New York: Metropolitan Museum of Art.

Barad, Karen. 2015. "On Touching: The Inhuman That Therefore I Am." In *The Politics of Materiality,* ed. Susanne Witzgall. http://gendersexualityfeminist.duke.edu/uploads/media_items/on-touching-the-inhuman-that-therefore-i-am-v1-1.original.pdf.

Barash, David P., and Judith Eve Lipton. 2001. *The Myth of Monogamy: Fidelity and Infidelity in Animals and People*. New York: Henry Holt.

Barber, Shannon. 2013. "Mexican Leader Says Gays Can't Marry Because They Don't Face Each Other While Having Sex." *Addicting Info*, August 19. http://addictinginfo .org/2013/08/19/mexican-leader-says-gays-cant-marry-because-they-dont-face -each-other-while-having-sex/.

Barthes, Roland. 1990. *A Lover's Discourse: Fragments*. London: Penguin.

———. 2012. *How to Live Together: Novelistic Simulations of Some Everyday Spaces*. New York: Columbia University Press.

Battan, Carrie. 2012. "Fiona Apple Writes an Open Letter Canceling Tour Dates, Asks for Blessings for Her Dying Dog Janet." *Pitchfork*, November. http://pitchfork.com/ news/48661-fiona-apple-writes-an-open-letter-canceling-tour-dates-asks-for -blessings-for-her-dying-dog-janet/.

Berger, John. 1991. "Why Look at Animals?" In *About Looking*. New York: Vintage.

Berlant, Lauren. 2011. *Cruel Optimism*. Durham, N.C.: Duke University Press.

———. 2012. *Desire/Love*. Brooklyn, N.Y.: Dead Letter Office/Punctum.

Bersani, Leo, and Ulysse Dutoit. 2008. *Forms of Being: Cinema, Aesthetics, Subjectivity*. London: BFI.

Bordeleau, Eric. 2013. "Soulful Sedentarity: Tsai Ming-Liang at Home at the Museum." *Studies in European Cinema* 10, nos. 2–3: 179–94.

Broglio, Ron. 2013. "After Animality, before the Law: Interview with Cary Wolfe." *Angelaki: Journal of the Theoretical Humanities* 18, no. 1: 181–89.

Bulkagov, Sergius. 2002. *The Bride of the Lamb*. Grand Rapids, Mich.: William B. Eerdmans.

Carson, Anne. 2014. "The Albertine Workout." *London Review of Books* 36, no. 11: 34–35.

Cary, Phillip. 2000. *Augustine's Invention of the Inner Self: The Legacy of a Christian Platonist*. Oxford: Oxford University Press.

Cherfas, Jeremy. 1977. "The Games Animals Play." *New Scientist*, September 15, 672–73.

Clark-Flory, Tracy. 2013. "The Truth about Female Desire: It's Base, Animalistic and Ravenous." *Salon*, June 1.

Clemens, Justin. 2013. "The Demon of Analogy: Simon O'Sullivan, *On the Production of Subjectivity*." *Parrhesia* 17: 72–75.

Coetzee, J. M. 2003. *Elizabeth Costello*. New York: Viking.

Combes, Muriel. 2012. *Gilbert Simondon and the Philosophy of the Transindividual*. Cambridge, Mass.: MIT Press.

Crocker, Lizzie. 2014. "Monster Porn Is the Latest Wrinkle in Self-Published Smut." *The Daily Beast*, January 14.

Daumal, René. 2012. *Pataphysical Essays*. Cambridge, Mass.: Wakefield Press.

Denby, David. 2009. "Brief Lives: *Notorious, Cherry Blossoms,* and *Wendy and Lucy*." *New Yorker*, January 26.

Derrida, Jacques. 2008. *The Animal That Therefore I Am*. New York: Fordham University Press.

———. 2009. *The Beast and the Sovereign*. Vol. 1. Chicago: Chicago University Press.

Dufourmantelle, Anne. 2007. *Blind Date: Sex and Philosophy*. Urbana: University of Illinois Press.

Eiseley, Loren. 1973. *The Immense Journey*. New York: Random House.

———. 1979. *The Star Thrower*. New York: Harvest.

———. 1997. "Instruments of Darkness." In *The Night Country*. Lincoln: University of Nebraska Press.

Flusser, Vilém. 2014. "The Gesture of Loving." In *Gestures*. Minneapolis: University of Minnesota Press.

Fourier, Charles. 1971. "The Nature and Uses of Love as Harmony." In *The Utopian Vision of Charles Fourier: Selected Texts on Work, Love, and Passionate Attraction*. New York: Beacon.

———. 2011. *The Hierarchies of Cuckoldry and Bankruptcy*. Cambridge, Mass.: Wakefield Press.

Fournival, Richard de. 2000. *Master Richard's Bestiary of Love and Response*. West Lafayette, Ind.: NotaBell Books.

Freud, Sigmund. 1955. "Group Psychology and the Analysis of the Ego." *Standard Edition* 18.

———. 1965. "The Dissection of the Psychical Personality." In *New Introductory Lectures on Psychoanalysis*, ed. James Strachey. New York: W. W. Norton.

Fromm, Erich. 1956. *The Art of Loving*. New York: Harper and Row.

Garnett, David. 1985. *"Lady into Fox" and "A Man in the Zoo."* London: Hogarth Press.

Gellman, Lindsay. 2014. "Tiger Photos Roam Wild on Online Dating Sites." *The Wall Street Journal*, May 26.

Gorfinkel, Elena. 2012. "Weariness, Waiting: Enduration and Art Cinema's Tired Bodies." *Discourse* 34, nos. 2–3: 311–47.

Gourmont, Remy de. 1922. *The Natural Philosophy of Love*. New York: Boni and Liveright.

Greenberg, Joel. 2014. Review of *The Animals: Love Letters between Christopher Isherwood and Don Bachardy*. *Sydney Morning Herald*, January 4–5, 30.

Greene, Jane Bannard, ed. 1969. *Letters of Rainer Maria Rilke, 1910–1926*. New York: W. W. Norton.

Grose, Francis. 1796. *A Classical Dictionary of the Vulgar Tongue*. London: Hooper.

Guérin, Maurice de. 1899. *"The Centaur" and "The Bacchante."* London: Hacon and Ricketts.

Halperin, David M. 2005. "Love's Irony: Six Remarks on Platonic Eros." In *Erotikon: Essays on Eros, Ancient and Modern*, ed. Shadi Bartsch and Thomas Bartscherer. Chicago: University of Chicago Press.

Haraway, Donna. 1991. "A Cyborg Manifesto." In *Simians, Cyborgs, and Women: The Reinvention of Nature*. New York: Routledge.

———. 2008. *When Species Meet*. Minneapolis: University of Minnesota Press.

Harman, Graham. 2002. *Tool-Being: Heidegger and the Metaphysics of Objects*. Chicago: Open Court.

Hazlitt, William. (1823) 2007. *Liber Amoris: or, The New Pygmalion*. Charleston, S.C.: BiblioBazaar.

Izmirlieva, Valentina. 2005. "Augustine Divided." In *Erotikon: Essays on Eros, Ancient and Modern*, ed. Shadi Bartsch and Thomas Bartscherer. Chicago: University of Chicago Press.

Keck, David. 1998. *Angels and Angelology in the Middle Ages*. Oxford: Oxford University Press.

Kinsey, Alfred. 1998. *Sexual Behavior in the Human Female*. Indianapolis: Indiana University Press.

Kohn, Eduardo. 2013. *How Forests Think: Toward an Anthropology beyond the Human*. Berkeley: University of California Press.

Law, Rachel, and McKenzie Wark. 2013. *W.A.N.T.: Weaponized Adorables Negotiation Team Book Project*. N.p.: Kickstarter.

Lemm, Vanessa. 2009. *Nietzsche's Animal Philosophy: Culture, Politics, and the Animality of the Human Being*. New York: Fordham University Press.

Lingis, Alphonso. 2003. "Animal Body, Inhuman Face." In *Zoontologies: The Question of the Animal*, ed. Cary Wolfe. Minneapolis: University of Minnesota Press.

Luhmann, Niklas. 2010. *Love: A Sketch*. Cambridge: Polity Press.

Malouf, David. 1981. *An Imaginary Life*. London: Picador.

McLuhan, Marshall. 1997. *War and Peace in the Global Village*. San Francisco: Hardwired.

Melville, Herman. 1922. *Moby Dick: or The White Whale*. Boston: St. Botolph Society.

Mitchell, Breon. 1990. Afterword to *Looking Back*, by Lou-Andreas Salomé. New York: Paragon House.

Morris, Desmond. 1989. *Horse Watching*. New York: Crown.

Morton, Timothy. 2012. *The Ecological Thought*. Cambridge, Mass.: Harvard University Press.

Most, Glenn W. 2005. "Six Remarks on Platonic Eros." In *Erotikon: Essays on Eros, Ancient and Modern*, ed. Shadi Bartsch and Thomas Bartscherer. Chicago: University of Chicago Press.

Musil, Robert. 1998. *Diaries: 1899–1941*. Edited by Mark Mirsky. New York: Basic Books.

———. 1999a. "Grigia." In *Five Women*. Boston: Verba Mundi.

———. 1999b. "The Perfecting of a Love." In *Five Women*. Boston: Verba Mundi.

———. 1999c. "The Temptation of Quiet Veronica." In *Five Women*. Boston: Verba Mundi.

———. 2006. *Posthumous Papers of a Living Author*. Brooklyn, N.Y.: Archipelago Books.

Nietzsche, Friedrich. 1989. *On the Genealogy of Morals*. New York: Vintage.

———. 1996a. *Human, All Too Human: A Book for Free Spirits*. Cambridge: Cambridge University Press.

———. 1996b. *Selected Letters of Friedrich Nietzsche*. Edited by Christopher Middleton. Chicago: University of Chicago Press.

Nussbaum, Martha C. 2005. "People as Fictions: Proust and the Ladder of Love." In *Erotikon: Essays on Eros, Ancient and Modern*, ed. Shadi Bartsch and Thomas Bartscherer. Chicago: University of Chicago Press.

O'Connell, Robert J. 1996. *Images of Conversion in St. Augustine's "Confessions."* New York: Fordham University Press.

O'Conner, Maureen. 2013. "The Women Who Write Dinosaur Erotica." *New York Magazine,* October 3.

O'Neill, John J. 1981. *Prodigal Genius: The Life of Nikola Tesla.* Los Angeles, Calif.: Angriff Press.

Oord, Thomas Jay. 2010. *Defining Love: A Philosophical, Scientific, and Theological Engagement.* Grand Rapids, Mich.: Brazos Press.

Ovid. 2002. *The Art of Love.* New York: The Modern Library.

——. 2004. *Metamorphoses.* London: Penguin Classics.

Peirce, Charles S. 1992. "Evolutionary Love." In *The Essential Peirce: Selected Philosophical Writings,* ed. Nathan Houser and Christian Kloesel, vol. 1, 1867–1893. Bloomington: Indiana University Press.

Peterson, Christopher. 2013. *Bestial Traces: Race, Sexuality, Animality.* New York: Fordham University Press.

Pettman, Dominic. 2002. *After the Orgy: Toward a Politics of Exhaustion.* New York: SUNY Press.

——. 2006. *Love and Other Technologies: Retrofitting Eros for the Information Age.* New York: Fordham University Press.

——. 2011. *Human Error: Species-Being and Media Machines.* Minneapolis: University of Minnesota Press.

——. 2013. *Look at the Bunny: Totem, Taboo, Technology.* Winchester, U.K.: Zero Books.

Pettman, Dominic, and Justin Clemens. 2004. "Relations with Concrete Others." In *Avoiding the Subject: Media, Culture and the Object.* Amsterdam: University of Amsterdam Press.

Pick, Anat. 2011. *Creaturely Poetics: Animality and Vulnerability in Literature and Film.* New York: Columbia University Press.

Plato. 1999. *The Symposium.* In *The Essential Plato.* New York: Quality Paperback Book Club.

Porter, James I. 2005. "Love of Life: Lucretius to Freud." In *Erotikon: Essays on Eros, Ancient and Modern,* ed. Shadi Bartsch and Thomas Bartscherer. Chicago: University of Chicago Press.

Pound, Ezra. 1922. "Translator's Postscript." In *The Natural Philosophy of Love,* ed. Remy de Gourmont (New York: Boni and Liveright, 1922).

Proctor, Hannah. 2014. "Reason Displaces All Love." *The New Inquiry,* February 14.

Proust, Marcel. 1982. *Swann's Way.* New York: Vintage.

——. 2006. *Remembrance of Things Past.* 2 vols. Hertfordshire, U.K.: Wordsworth Editions.

Reboux, Paul. 2004. *Les Animaux et l'Amour.* Paris: Mille et Une Nuits.

Rich, Joel. 2005. "Proust among the Animals." Lecture, University of Chicago, December 2. http://www.proustian.com/.

Rilke, Rainer Maria. 1984. Introduction to *Mitsou,* by Balthus. New York: Metropolitan Museum of Art.

——. 2009. *"The Duino Elegies" and "Sonnets to Orpheus."* New York: Vintage.

Rowland, Beryl. 1973. *Animals with Human Faces: A Guide to Animal Symbolism.* Knoxville: University of Tennessee Press.

Ryan, Judith. 1999. *Rilke, Modernism and Poetic Tradition.* Cambridge: Cambridge University Press.

Sade, Marquis de. 1990. *"Justine," "Philosophy in the Bedroom," and Other Writings.* New York: Grove Press.

Santner, Eric L. 2006. *On Creaturely Life: Rilke, Benjamin, Sebald.* Chicago: University of Chicago Press.

Sax, Boria. 1998. *The Serpent and the Swan: The Animal Bride in Folklore and Literature.* Blacksburg, Va.: McDonald and Woodward.

Shaviro, Steven. 2002. "The Erotic Life of Machines." *Parallax* 8, no. 4: 21–31.

Silverman, Kaja. 2009. *Flesh of My Flesh.* Palo Alto, Calif.: Stanford University Press.

Simondon, Gilbert. 2011. *Two Lessons on Animal and Man.* Minneapolis, Minn.: Univocal.

Stiegler, Bernard. 2010. *Taking Care of Youth and the Generations.* Palo Alto, Calif.: Stanford University Press.

———. 2012. "Relational Ecology and the Digital *Pharmakon*." *Culture Machine* 13: 1–19.

———. 2015. *States of Shock: Stupidity and Knowledge in the 21st Century.* Cambridge: Polity.

Thacker, Eugene. 2009. "The Anchorite and the Somnambulist: Four Theses towards a New Theory of Solipsism." *Journal of Comparative Theology* 22, no. 12: 29–42.

———. 2010. *After Life.* Chicago: University of Chicago Press.

———. 2013. "Apophatic Animality: Lautréamont, Bachelard, and the Bliss of Metamorphosis." *Angelaki* 18, no. 1: 83–98.

Thiher, Allen. 2009. *Understanding Robert Musil.* Columbia: University of South Carolina Press.

Tracy, David. 2005. "The Divided Consciousness of Augustine on Eros." In *Erotikon: Essays on Eros, Ancient and Modern,* ed. Shadi Bartsch and Thomas Bartscherer. Chicago: University of Chicago Press.

Uexküll, Jakob von. 2010. *"A Foray into the Worlds of Animals and Humans," with "A Theory of Meaning."* Minneapolis: University of Minnesota Press.

Vaillancourt, Tracy. 2013. "Do Human Females Use Indirect Aggression as an Intrasexual Competition Strategy?" *Philosophical Transactions of the Royal Society* 368, no. 1631.

Vincent, Alice. 2014. "The Rejection Letters: How Publishers Snubbed 11 Great Authors." *The Telegraph,* June 5.

Wolfe, Cary. 2013. "After Animality, before the Law: Interviewed by Ron Broglio." *Angelaki* 18, no. 1: 181–89.

Wolfenstein, Eugene Victor. 2000. *Inside/outside Nietzsche: Psychoanalytic Explorations.* Ithaca, N.Y.: Cornell University Press.

# INDEX

Acteaon, metamorphosis of, 80, 136n2

Adam and Eve, 10, 58, 89

Adamson, Joy, 95

adultery. *See* cuckold

Aesop's fables: *Bestiality of Love* and, 58

affective heritage, x, 109–10

Agamben, Giorgio, 8, 41, 44, 85–91, 137n6, 139n5, 141n5; "anthropological machine," 8, 41, 42, 94–95, 110, 137n6; on Hellenic mystery cults, 138n2; on human desire for recognition, 93–94, 118, 140n3; on love of an *imago*, 86–87; on nymphs, 85–87, 89, 104, 140n2; objection to biometrics, 140n3; on readings of the Open, 129n2; vision of the end-of-history, 88

*agape* and *eros*, Christian distinction between, 5, 125n3

Agathon, 108

Agostinelli, Alfred, 134n3

Aibo (robot dog), 102–3, 104

Alcibiades, 140n4

alienation, human, 20; in *Her*, 100–101

allegorical animals, 56

"All Is Full of Love" (Björk), 143n11

alterity, alien aspect of, 39

analogy(ies): importance to self-perception and self-conception, 55; between individuated entities, 82–83; as literal, 108; as metaphysics

wearing a mask, 82; Musil on, 133n4; Silverman's sense of, 34, 82, 107–8, 130nn5–6, 131n7

Andersen, Hans Christian, 137n2

Andreas, Friedrich Carl, 19

Andreas-Salomé, Lou, 128n12; appreciation of animality, 19–20; centaurs and, 24; *marriage blanc* of, 15–21, 23, 127n9; Nietzsche's sister, Elizabeth, on, 18–19; pilgrimage to Russia of, 20–21; Rilke and, 19, 20–21, 23, 25, 129nn14–15, 130n5

angel(s): centaurs and, 17–18; dialectic between beast and, 33–34; in Keck's emotionology, 126n4; Rilke between animal and, 22–25, 129n15

animal bride story, 47, 66–72, 137nn2–3; subtextual moral of, 66–67, 77; as totem ancestor, 67–68

animal culture and communication, 89

animal groom stories, 136n1

animal magnetism, 114–19

"animal question," ix

animals: encounters with machines, 143n12; estrangement from actual, 97–99, 101–5; humans as "clothed animals," Agamben on, 91; mediated experiences with, 98–99; and social network feeds, 97–98; women and wild/exotic, 95

bull: Jupiter as, 74–75; in story of Pasiphaë, 75–76

Bunny, Rupert, 140n2

Burroughs, William, x

Byblis, Ovid's story of, 78–79

Callisto (nymph), 139n3

Canepari, Zackary, 102

capitalism, love within libidinal economy and, 49, 61, 72, 86, 92–93, 102, 136n3, 138n5

*Captive, The* (Proust), 47

capture and captivation, 50–54

*caritas* versus *cupiditas*, 125n3

Carson, Anne, 134n3

Cary, Phillip, 125n1

*Cat of the Mediterranean* (Balthus), 28

cats, 18; Balthus and Mitsou, 26–29, 42; Musil on, 42–43; Rilke on, 27, 28

centaur, 17–18, 23–24, 127nn7–8; Proust's M. de Charlus as, 46; socioeconomic, invention of stirrup and, 127n6

"Centaur, Le" (Guérin), 24

Chamberlain, Neville, 40

*charivari*, 138n10

Cherfas, Jeremy, 136n4

Chiron (centaur), 18, 127n8

Christian discourse: *agape* and *eros*, distinction between, 5, 125n3; Creator–creature distinction in, 125n1; creaturely love in, 9–12, 125n2

Cinderella story, 137n2

civilization, eros and, 5

Clark-Flory, Tracy, 130n3

class: in Musil's depictions of women, 131n8; selection of sexual partners by, 136n3

Clemens, Justin, 124n2, 143n11

clothed animal, humans as the, 91, 141n6

cockatrice, 62–64

Coetzee, J. M., 138n10

Combes, Muriel, 140n8, 146n17

companionship, pattern recognition and need for, 51–52

Constantinople, Council of (A.D. 381), 125n1

continuity-within-difference, in Ovid's universe, 80–81

Cooper, Drea, 102

courtesans, 64–65

courtly love, 57

*Cranes Are Flying, The* (film), 145n11

Creator–creature distinction, canonical notion of, 125n1

creature(s): creaturely continuum inhabited by humans, 19; within creaturely poetics, Pick on, 127n11; definitions from *OED*, 12; equation with nonhuman realm of universal creation, 128n12; "good," 126n4; importance to Victorians, 11; mythical, 17–18; in Proust's universe, 44–49, 133n2; uses of term, 7, 9, 44, 70, 91, 136n2; Western disavowal of our creaturely life, 7–8

*Creaturely Life* (Santner), 128n13, 144n7

creaturely love, xi, 2, 128n13; beloved as fusion of both Beast and Sovereign in, 144n7; creaturely hate behind, 60; divine aspect of, 9–10, 12; in *Libor Amoris*, 63; in *Metamorphoses*, 82; Musil's depiction of, 33–37, 131n9; non-Western versus Western myth of, 67; as oxymoron, 111; Tesla's love of pigeons, 114–18; in theological debates, 9–12, 125n2; as virtual familiar in Proust, 49

"creaturely poetics," Pick's notion of, 127n11

critter, Haraway's use of term, 146n16

Crocker, Lizzie, 130n3

cross-dressing, 77

cross-species romance, 66–72

cuckold: cockatrice and, 62–64; Fourier on, 60–64, 65, 132n1; in nature, 62; origin of word, 60; symbols of, 60, 136nn1–2; taxonomy of, 61–62

Cukor, George, 145n11

culture: animal, 89; reduction to biology and evolution of, 94, 140n3

Cupid, 68; arrows of, 74

cute animal phenomenon, 98–99, 142n3

"cybernetic triangle," 14, 118

cybersex, Ovid's prophetic vision of, 99–100

"Cyborg Manifesto" (Haraway), 146n18
Cyparíssus's love of stag, in Ovid, 139n6

Daphne, metamorphosis of, 81
Darwin, Charles, 11, 36
*Dasein*, 83, 129n2
Dasent, George, 136n1
dating sites, 99, 142n5
Daumal, René, 145n14
death, 131n7; characteristic shared by all
    creatures, 24, 108, 118–19; god's envy
    of our finitude, 138n1; love's final irony
    and, 144n4; ultimate metamorphosis
    of, 84
Debord, Guy, 87
De Landa, Manuel, 83
Deleuze, Gilles, 5, 83, 107, 113, 127n6,
    143n14; desiring machine, 124n2,
    143n14; use of term desire, 123n2
Denby, David, 94
Derrida, Jacques, 88, 91, 127n8, 133n2,
    141nn7–8, 144n7; on auto-deixis, 54; on
    hetero-narcissism, 135n7; on human-
    ism and "symbolic" thought, 144n7; on
    marionettes, 130n5
desire, xi, 3–7, 123n3; through analogy,
    Silverman on, 34; anthropocentric
    ambivalence in discourse on, 110–11;
    author's use of term, 124n2; coded as
    physical, 6; female, in *Metamorphoses*,
    75–78; love as one form of, 3–4;
    metamorphoses triggered by, 73;
    Musil's search for secret and source of,
    42, 131n9; paradox produced by, 3–4;
    protean nature of, recognizing, 65; for
    recognition, 93–94, 118, 140n3
*Desire/Love* (Berlant), 3–4
desiring machines, posthuman, 105,
    124n2, 143n14
*Digital Dionysus* (Mellamphy and
    Mellamphy), 126n1
dinosaur erotica, 130n3
Diotima, 108–9
*Diplozoon paradoxum* (flatworm),
    monogamy of, 136n4
Disney, 98

"Divided Consciousness of Augustine on
    Eros, The" (Tracy), 125n3
dog: Aibo, 102–3, 104; love for, 130n1,
    141nn1–3; love for, in *Wendy and Lucy*,
    12, 92–96, 112–13, 141nn1–2; love for, in
    *Temptations of Quiet Veronica*, 35–37;
    sexual habits of, 71
"Do Human Females Use Indirect Aggres-
    sion as an Intrasexual Competition
    Strategy?" (Vaillancourt), 136n4
domestication: animal bride story and, 66;
    animal totems and, 99; wolves and, 72.
    *See also* pets
Donne, John, 135n1
Donner, Richard, 67
drive (human), distinction between
    (animal) instinct and, 109
Dufourmantelle, Anne, 18, 19, 143n2,
    143n14
*Duino* (Rilke), 21, 23
Dutoit, Ulysse, 73, 110, 143n3, 146n15

Echo, 75, 81
Edison, Thomas, 114, 115
Edison Prize, 115
ego, coextensive with environment, 36
Eiseley, Loren, 109–10, 123n1, 139n4,
    139n6, 140n12, 144n4
electrical currents, 114
Electrical Engineers Club, 115
*Elizabeth Costello* (Coetzee), 138n1
Emerson, Ralph Waldo, 139n6
emotionology, 126n4
empathy, 82
Enlightenment, 71, 104
*eros*: *agape* and, Christian distinction
    between, 5, 125n3; non-sexual, Musil
    on residual need for, 43; in *Symposium*,
    108; zoological approach to, in *Bestiary
    of Love*, 56
eroticism, 5–6, 108
Eryximachus, 108
evolution, 48, 50
evolutionary biology, 136n4
"Evolutionary Love" (Peirce), 126n5
exceptionalism: human, 19, 23, 62, 88–89,

128nn12–13, 129n2; of the symbolic, 144n7

exhibitionism, 141n7

extimacy, 3

Fabre, Jean-Henri, 41

fairy tales: animal bride/groom stories as purest, 69–70; wolf in "Little Red Riding Hood," 72

*Family Dog, The* (film), 102–3

*Fathers and Sons* (Turgenev), 42

faunification, 89

femininity, as impossible performance, 94–95

feminism, 64, 132n1

fingerprinting, recognition by, 93–94

finitude. *See* death

"Flea, The" (Donne), 135n1

*Flesh of My Flesh* (Silverman), 130n5

Flusser, Vilém, 6

Ford, Harrison, 141n1

Forel, Auguste-Henri, 41

forgetting of Being, 32

Fossey, Dian, 95, 96

Fourier, Charles, 12, 60–65, 66, 132n1; on cuckoldry, 60–64, 65, 132n1; on "phalanstery," 61, 64; on women as victims of society's hypocrisy, 64

Fournival, Richard de, 12, 55–59, 141n6

*Frankenstein* (Shelley), 11

*Frantic* (film), 141n1

Freud, Sigmund, 34, 36, 43, 81, 124n2; on horse as totemic creature, 17, 126n4; incest taboo and, 78; on libido and desire–love distinction, 4–5, 17

friendship, love and, 6

"Frog King, The" (fairy tale), 70

Fromm, Erich, 123n2

Funabashi, Hiroshi, 102

fur, 28, 37; totemic power of, 39, 132n1

Galen, 144n6

Garnett, David, 137n3

Gellman, Lindsay, 142n4

gender: female sexuality, 130n3; as great existential divide, 66–67, 77

gendered intercourse, natural law of, 78

*Genealogy of Morals* (Nietzsche), 16

generic, the, 140n11

genocide, 42

Gleik, James, 142n7

Global Financial Crisis, love in wake of, 93

goat: in the machine, 105, 143n13; medieval distrust of, 71

God, love of, 10, 46

gods: envy of human's finitude, 138n1; modesty of, 89–90; sex between mortals and, 68, 73, 74–75, 138nn1–2

Goodall, Jane, 95

"good creatures," 126n4

Gorfinkel, Elena, 141n2

grace, 141n5; creaturely love rendered sacred by, 11

Great Chain of Being, x, 19

Great War, 11, 26

Greenberg, Joel, 133n5

Greene, Jane Bannard, 24

"Grigia" (Musil), 131n8

Grose, Francis, 136n1

Guattari, Félix, 113, 124n2

Guérin, Maurice de, 24

Halperin, David M., 144n4

Haraway, Donna, 33, 112, 138n3, 139n7, 146n16, 146n18

hare, as symbol of libidinousness, 137n8

Harkness, Ruth, 95

Harman, Graham, 140n13

Hazlitt, William, 62–63

Hegel, Georg Wilhelm Friedrich, 50

Heidegger, Martin, 32, 50, 83, 89, 97, 129n2

Hellenic mystery cults, 138n2

Hepburn, Audrey, 144n11

*Her* (film), 12, 100–102, 142nn6–7

hermaphrodite, origin of term, 76

Hermaphroditus, Salmacis and, 76–77

hetero-narcissism, Derrida on, 135n7

*Hierarchies of Bankruptcy, The,* 61

*Hierarchies of Cuckoldry, The* (Fourier), 60–62, 63–64, 65

Hinge (dating site), 99

Kafka, Franz, 111, 128n13
"kawaii" creatures, 97, 142n3
Keck, David, 11, 126n4
Kermode, Frank, 30
Kilmartin, Terence, 133n2
Kinsey, Alfred, 144n6
Klossowska, Elizabeth, 26
Kohn, Eduardo, 137n5, 145n13

Lacan, Jacques, 3, 5, 7, 28, 67, 124n2; use of
    term desire, 3, 5, 123n2
Laclos, Pierre Choderlos de, 59
*Ladyhawke* (film), 67
*Lady into Fox* (Garnett), 137n3
language: of courtly love in *Bestiary of
    Love*, 57–59; creaturely poetics, 127n11;
    human capacity for, 50; nymphs'
    possession of, 86; of Proust, to describe
    creature, 44–45; Rilke's Open occurring
    outside walls of, 22, 129n2
Laurence, William L., 118
Lautréamont, Comte de, 144n9
Law, Rachel, 142n3
Lawrence, D. H., 33
Lee, Ang, 142n5
Leibniz, G. W., 83
Lemm, Vanessa, 17–18
Lévi-Strauss, Claude, 17, 67, 78
libido: attraction to bestiality, in "Perfect-
    ing of a Love," 31–33; Freud on, 4–5,
    17; libidinal ecology, 33, 36; libidinal
    economy of sexual commerce, 49, 61,
    72, 86, 92–93, 102, 136n3, 138n5; texture
    of fur as trigger for, 39, 132n1
*Libor Amoris* (Hazlitt), 62–63
*Life of Pi, The* (Martel), 142n5
Lingis, Alphonso, 146n20
Linnaeus, Carl, 41
Lipton, Judith Eve, 136n4
Little Hans, case of, 17
*Little Mermaid, The* (Andersen), 137n2
"Little Red Riding Hood," 72
"living thought," Kohn on, 137n5
*Lolita* (Nabokov), 27
*Look at the Bunny* (Pettman), 126n3
love: animalistic origins of, in *Art of Love*,

90–91; attraction versus, ix, 2; as
catalytic trauma in *Metamorphoses*,
74–78; courtly, 57; definitions of, 2–7,
107, 119, 123n2; desire and, distinction
between, xi, 3–7; final irony of, 144n4;
as force animating all animated things,
144n5; of an *imago*, Agamben on,
86–87; mutual, 68, 103, 113, 118;
navigation and, 100; passionate, Proust
on, 45–49, 50; of pets, 26–29, 92–96;
posthuman, 102–5, 124n2, 143n14;
protean nature of the beloved, 81;
Rilke's Open and epiphanic shock
of, 22–23; in *Symposium*, 108–9; as
technology, 97–105; unconditional,
12; unrequited, 74. *See also* creaturely
love
*Love and Other Technologies* (Pettman),
    124n3
"Love in the Time of Tamagotchi" (Pett-
    man), 143n11
"love plot," 3, 4
*Lovers Discourse, A* (Barthes), 124n4
"love tone," 52
Lucretius, 144n5
Luhmann, Niklas, 3
lust, xi, 30

machinic companions, 102–4, 143n11. *See
    also* technology
Maeterlinck, Maurice, 40
magnetism, animal, 114–19
Malouf, David, 84
*Man without Qualities, The* (Musil), 30,
    132n2
Marcovaldi, Martha, 38–40; the Raven, 40
marionettes, 130n5
marriage: animal bride, 47, 66–72,
    137nn2–3; carceral aspect of wedlock,
    61; Fourier on cuckoldry, 60–64, 65,
    132n1; *Libor Amoris* and the cockatrice,
    62–63; Musil's analogy between married
    people and animals, 40; ring as symbol
    in, 72; similarity between romantic love
    and pet-keeping and, 68; swans as role
    models for, 62

marriage blanc, of Nietzsche, Andreas-
    Salomé, and Rée, 15–21, 23, 127n9
Martel, Yann, 142n5
McLuhan, Marshall, 87, 127n6
*Mechanical Love* (film), 102
melancholia, 109
Mellamphy, Dan, 126n1
Mellamphy, Nandita Biswas, 126n1
Melusine (mermaid-figure), 47
Melville, Herman, 106–7, 143n1
meta-instinctual animal life, 53–54
*Metamorphoses* (Ovid), 73–82, 85, 127n7,
    138nn5–6; continuity-within-difference
    in, 80–81; female desire in, 75–78; incest
    in, 78–79; love as catalytic trauma
    in, 74–78; male duplicity in, 74–75;
    metaphor literally transfigured in, 82;
    triggers of change in, 73–74
metamorphosis: of death, 84; triggered by
    love, 73; of Zeus, 68
metaphor: analogy versus, 130n6;
    anthropocentric ambivalence and
    reliance on, 110–11; in *Bestiary of Love,*
    57; creaturely, to describe love, 137n3;
    literally transfigured in *Metamorphoses,*
    82; Nietzsche's use of, to describe
    Salomé, 18
metaphysics, 83–84; Ovid's fickle, 80–82,
    84, 139nn1–4
Middle Ages: *Bestiary of Love,* 55–59, 66;
    medieval bestiary, genre of, 70–71
Minotaur, 76
mirror effect, hetero-narcissism and, 135n7
Mitchell, Breon, 15, 128n12
*Mitsein* (being-with), 112
Mitsou, Balthus and, 26–29, 42
Möbius strip, love and desire forming, 6–7
*Moby Dick* (Melville), 106–7
modernists, 12; Andreas-Salomé, questions
    asked by, 13. *See also* Balthus; Musil,
    Robert; Nietzsche, Friedrich; Proust,
    Marcel; Rilke, Rainier Maria
modesty, sense of, 89–90, 141n7
Moncrieff, Scott, 133n2
monogamy, 62, 136n4; promise of,
    Nietzsche on, 64–65. *See also* marriage

Montaigne, Michel de, 69
morality, 64–65; incest taboo, 78–79;
    mapping of species as form of, 107;
    symbolic import of medieval bestiary,
    70–71
Morris, Desmond, 127n6
Morton, Timothy, 112, 140n10
Most, Glenn, 127n9
Müller, Alfred, 40
Musil, Martha, 132n3
Musil, Robert, 12, 30–37, 42, 130nn1–2,
    132nn1–3, 133nn6–7; depictions
    of women, 131n8; diary of, 39–43,
    134n1; fascination with dead sister,
    132n2; hybrid approach to writing, 30;
    "The Perfecting of a Love," 30–33; as
    poet laureate of ambivalence, 31; on
    souls, 38; "The Temptations of Quiet
    Veronica," 30, 33–37, 38, 131nn8–9;
    unfinished projects, 40–41; upbringing,
    130n2; women influencing writings of,
    38–40
mutual love, 68, 103, 113, 118
Myrrha, incestual passion of, 78–79, 80
mythical creatures, 17–18

Nabokov, Vladimir, x, 134n1
narcissism, 36, 38, 46, 140n11; exhibition
    of, 54, 135n7
Narcissus, 81, 89
nature: conflicting role of, 79; cuckold in,
    62; machinic nature of, 84; as queer
    heterotopia, 78; Uexküll and, 135n4
negentropic mystery of life, 104
Nicea, Council of (A.D. 325), 125n1
Nietzsche, Friedrich, xi, 12, 15–19, 64–65,
    126n2; animal philosophy, 17–19; fable
    of insanity of, 16; *marriage blanc* of,
    15–21, 23, 127n9; service with Prus-
    sian artillery division, 16–17; sister,
    Elisabeth, on Salomé, 18–19; vision of
    the human, 24
*nomos* and *phusis*, breach between, 78, 94
"non-ratiod" state, Musil on, 39
Not-Nothing, 83
"Nudity" (Agamben), 141n5

priest, animal equated with, 33–34
Proctor, Hannah, 136n3
*Prodigal Genius* (O'Neill), 114
Proust, Marcel, 12, 44–49, 50, 89, 133n1,
    134n3; creature in universe of, 44–49,
    133n2; jealousy in, 44, 47–49; search
    image of, perception images within, 52
"Proust among the Animals" (Rich), 134n6
Pseudo-Dionysius, 107
psyche, Bailly's view of, 53
psychoanalysis, 4–5, 20, 123n2; alteration
    of, in libidinal ecology, 36; *Metamor-*
    *phoses* and, 81. *See also* Freud, Sigmund
puppets, 130n5
Pythagoras, 80, 81, 139nn1–2

rabbit *(cuniculus)*, association with vagina
    *(cunnus)*, 137n8
race, in creaturely discourse, 143n1
Reboux, Paul, 1–2, 123n1
recognition: Hegelian dialectic of mutual,
    103; human desire for, 93–94, 118,
    140n3; need for companionship and,
    51–52
Rée, Paul, 15, 127n9; *marriage blanc* of,
    15–21, 23, 127n9
Reichardt, Kelly, 12, 92, 94, 141n1
remembering of Being, 6, 32
repeatable being, Bersani on, 143n3
Rich, Joel, 134n6
Rilke, Rainier Maria, 12, 22–29, 38, 128n13,
    130n1; between animal and angel,
    22–25, 129n3, 129n15; Balthus and
    Mitsou, 26–29, 42; on cats, 27, 28; on
    the Open, 22–23, 25, 38, 129n2; Salomé
    and, 19, 20–21, 23, 25, 129nn14–15,
    130n5
ritual and improvisation, 53
robots, 102–4. *See also* technology
romance: ambiguity of early genre, 57;
    bestiary lore and epistolary, Fournival's
    splicing of, 55–59; cross-species, 66–72;
    and the hunt, 68, 135n2; Zalkind's on,
    136n3
Romanes, J. G., 40

Rowland, Beryl, 70, 71–72, 136n2,
    137nn7–8, 138n9
Ryan, Judith, 24

Sacher-Masoch, Leopold von, 132n1
Sade, Marquis de, 135n2
Sagan, Dorion, 51
Salmacis, Ovid's story of, 76–77
Salomé, 12, 129n3, 129n15. *See also*
    Andreas-Salomé, Lou
Santner, Eric L., 127n11, 128n13, 144n7
satyr, 71; faunification of, 89
Sax, Boria, 66–69, 136n1, 137n2; on animal
    bride, 66, 67–68; on our animal origins,
    137n6
*Schadenfreude* and *Schadennietzsche,*
    126n5
Schloss Bergam Irchel (castle), Rilke at,
    129n15
Scholastics, 83, 140n9
Schultze, Fritz, 41
scold's bridle, 72, 138n10
search image, Uexküll's perception image
    and, 51–52
Sebald, W. G., 128n13
self: analogy and, 55; auto-deixis, 54;
    creaturely love and sense of, 33, 35–37;
    defining sense of, 133n8; metamorpho-
    ses troubling identity in Ovid, 74, 80
self-alienation, biometrics and, 94
self-consciousness, 89, 91
selfish gene, 2
*Sexual Behavior in the Human Female*
    (Kinsey), 144n6
sexual fulfillment, 88
sexual intercourse: as bestiality, 90, 146n20;
    between gods and mortals, 68, 73,
    74–75, 138nn1–2; riding as term for,
    138n9; unhuman aspect of, 137n7
sexual mechanism, continuum between
    creaturely and human, 124n4
Shakespeare, William, 126n4
shame, human sense of, 89, 141n7
Shaviro, Steven, 143n11
Shelley, Mary, 11

Silverman, Kaja, 21, 23, 127n10, 143n3; on analogy, 34, 82, 107–8, 130nn5–6, 131n7
Simondon, Gilbert, 32, 83, 140n8, 146n17
Sirens, 56–57
Siri (iPhone), 100
"sneaky fucker" strategy of beta males, 136n4
social network feeds, prevalence of animals in, 97–98. *See also* Internet; technology
Socrates, 108–9, 140n4, 145n14
*Sodom and Gomorrah* (Proust), 45, 46–47, 134n4
sodomy, 33
*Sonic Intimacy* (Pettman), 142n6
soul: Aristotle's definition of, 146n19; belief in metaphoric or allegorical human, 104; indestructability of, 80, 81; mechanical equivalent of vegetative, 104; Musil on, 30, 33, 38, 39–40; nymphs' lack of, 86; of object, Japanese belief in, 102–3; Socrates' concept of, 145n14; transmigration of, 118, 139n6
"Soulful Sedentarity" (Bordeleau), 140n8
spectacle: animal as, 98; for different perceptual systems, 109–10, 144n8; viewing the human in age of intensified, 144n11
Sphinx, 145n14
Spinoza, 83, 133n1, 143n14
stags: cuckold's horns and mating habits of, 60; Cyparíssus's love of, in Ovid, 139n6
Stiegler, Bernard, 8, 110, 145n12, 146n17
stirrup, invention of, 127n6
"Substance and Shadow" (James), 126n5
superego, 17
surplus, Deleuzians' view of desire as cosmic, 123n2
swans: as gods' disguise, 68, 73, 138n1; Proust's real-life use of, as totem, 134n3; as role models for marriage, 62
symbolic, exceptionalism of the, 144n7
symbolism, animal, 16–18, 137n5; animal bride stories, 47, 66–72, 137nn2–3; in Enlightenment, 71; horns, 60–61,

136nn1–2; whale in *Moby Dick,* 106. *See also* animal totems
*Symposium* (Plato), 88, 108–9, 140n4

taboo sexual practices, 33–37; incest, 78–79
Tamagotchi virtual pets, 102
Tarde, Gabriel, 83
Tarr, Béla, 16
taxonomy, 83–84
technology: disguised as animals, 102; interspecies war machine, 127n6; love as, 97–105; patagraphy, 145n14; *pharmakon* as descriptor for, 110, 145n12; role of, 13–14; technical clairvoyance, 98
Teiresias, 77
"Temptations of Quiet Veronica, The" (Musil), 30, 33–37, 38, 131nn8–9
Tesla, Nikola, 114–19; award of Edison Prize, 115; love of pigeons, 114–18
Thacker, Eugene, 140n9, 140n11, 144n9
theological debates, creaturely love in, 9–12, 125n2
*Theory of the Four Movements and the General Destinies* (Fourier), 61
Thiher, Allen, 31, 34, 130n2, 130n4, 131n8
Thurn und Taxis-Hohenlohe, Princess Marie von, 24
Tinder (dating site), 99
Titian, 140n2
Tolstoy, Leo, 20
Topsell, Edward, 71
totemism, 16–19, 23, 40, 126n3, 133n5, 134n3, 134n5; animal bride as totem ancestor, 67–68; domesticated creatures and, 99; in *Her*, 100–102; totemic power of fur, 39, 132n1
touch, physics of, 130n2
Tracy, David, 10, 125n3
transductive unity, 140n8
transgendered figure, 76–77
transindividuation, 32, 146n17
transitivity of being, 6–7
transmigration of souls, 139n6
Trier, Lars Von, 140n1

Turgenev, Ivan, 42
*Turin Horse, The* (film), 16
"Twelve Commandments for the Sexual
    Revolution of the Proletariat" (Zalkind),
    136n3

Uexküll, Jakob von, 51–52, 134n2, 134n4
*Umberto D.* (film), 141n1
*Umwelt* (environment), 51–52, 53, 55, 111,
    134n3
unconditional love, 12
*Unions* (Musil), 30
unrequited love, 74

vagina *(cunnus)*, rabbit *(cuniculus)* associ-
    ated with, 137n8
Vaillancourt, Tracy, 136n4
*Venus in Furs* (Sacher-Masoch), 132n1
Victorians: importance of creature to, 11;
    sense of omniscience, 40
Vincent, Alice, 106
virtual girlfriends, 143n11
virtual pets, 102
Vogt, Carl, 40

Wakefield Press, 61
*Wall Street Journal,* 99
Wark, McKenzie, 142n3
Weil, Simone, 128n11
*Wendy and Lucy* (film), 12, 92–96, 112–13,
    141nn1–2

Western tradition, animals in, 13–14
Westinghouse Corporation, 114
whale, in *Moby Dick,* 106
*What Do Women Want?* (Bergner), 130n3
Whitehead, Alfred North, 83, 144n4
whore, origin of word, 137n8
Wilde, Olivia, 100
Williams, Michelle, 92, 94, 141n1
witches, women tried and executed as, 69
*Within a Budding Grove* (Proust), 47
Wolfe, Cary, 135n5
Wolfenstein, Eugene Victor, 127n9
Wolff, Kurt, 27
wolves, 72
women: female sexuality as animalistic,
    130n3; femininity and, 94–95; Fourier
    on cuckold and cockatrice, 60–64, 65,
    132n1; love between creature and,
    94–95; in *Metamorphoses,* 75–77;
    nymphomania, 86, 140n1; solidarity of
    sisterhood, 59; two Marys composing
    dialectic representation of, 58; as
    victims of society's hypocrisy, Fourier
    on, 64
*Women, The* (film), 145n11
*World of Wonder* (BBC), 134n3
Wundt, Wilhelm, 41

Zalkind, Aron, 136n3
Zarathustra, 127n10
Zeus, metamorphoses of, 68

(continued from page ii)

**DOMINIC PETTMAN** is professor of culture and media at Eugene Lang College at the New School for Social Research. He is the author of many books, including *Love and Other Technologies: Retrofitting Eros for the Information Age*; *Human Error: Species-Being and Media Machines* (Minnesota, 2011); *Look at the Bunny: Totem, Taboo, Technology*; *Infinite Distraction: Paying Attention to Social Media*; and *Sonic Intimacy: Voice, Species, Technics*.